Anna D'Almeida

A Lady's Visit to Manilla and Japan

Anna D'Almeida

A Lady's Visit to Manilla and Japan

ISBN/EAN: 9783337184223

Printed in Europe, USA, Canada, Australia, Japan

Cover: Foto ©Andreas Hilbeck / pixelio.de

More available books at **www.hansebooks.com**

A LADY'S VISIT
TO
MANILLA AND JAPAN.

A JAPANESE "TEA-HOUSE" GIRL

BY

ANNA D'Almeida

LONDON:
HURST AND BLACKETT, PUBLISHERS,
SUCCESSORS TO HENRY COLBURN,
13, GREAT MARLBOROUGH STREET.
1863.
The right of Translation is reserved.

TO THEE,

WHO HAST AIDED ME IN MY TOILS,

AND SO KINDLY SMOOTHED EVERY DIFFICULT PATH AND RUGGED STEP,

IS DEDICATED

THIS LITTLE WORK

BY

THY LOVING AND FAITHFUL WIFE,

ANNA.

PREFACE.

In launching my small craft on the wide sea of Literature, I must be permitted to prepare my readers, by one or two prefatory remarks, for what they may expect on the distant voyage which, under my guidance, they are about to undertake. The vessel in which I invite them to accompany me, is not one of vast dimensions, fitted out for some great and important service, but a little bark, adapted only for a summer sea, in which I hope they may enjoy with me all the *agrémens* of a pleasure sail, and while away a few hours in light, but, I trust, not unprofitable amusement.

To be more explicit—for which purpose I must drop the language of metaphor—no one need expect to find in these pages the results of scientific research, or tedious disquisitions on the ethnology and early history of the country. My little work, which has no such ambitious aim, professes only to represent Japan and its people as they exist at the present moment. It contains an account of the various places which, during a cruise of some months in Japanese waters, I had the pleasure of visiting, with characteristic sketches of the peculiar race inhabiting these distant islands, and amusing anecdotes illustrative of their manners and customs.

I have purposely avoided all allusion to political matters, not having sufficient confidence in the correctness of my own judgment to justify me in assuming the office of a public instructor. In Japan the *arcana imperii* are so fenced round, and guarded, by the mystery with which the jealous fears of the rulers invest them—the affairs of state are so cautiously, and I may even say covertly, conducted—that a foreigner, in the course of his intercourse with this interesting people, finds it impossible to glean more than the most vague and uncertain information. Others, more able than I, have touched upon this subject, whether satisfactorily or not, you—the Great Public—know best.

The frontispiece to this work is from a sketch taken on the spot by my husband, and finished by Mr. Benjamin Barker, of Bath.

CONTENTS.

CHAPTER I.

Leave Singapore for Hong Kong—Life on Board—Arrive at Victoria—Ascend the Peak—Go to Manilla—Wretched Three Days' Voyage—Filthy Steamer — Manilla Bay — Custom-House—Hotel—A Drive to hear the Band—Fires—Landlady's Suggestions as to the Cause of them—Bigotry of the Inhabitants—Taxes—Description of the Town—Statue of the Queen—Origin of the Name of Luzon—Description of a Native Woman—Barracks and Prison—Uses of the Bamboo—Buffaloes very numerous—Mangoes—Chocolate . . . 3

CHAPTER II.

The Cathedral—Curious Pictures—Old Legend of Saint Christopher—Visit to the Cemetery—Tales—Cigar Manufactory—Description of Tagalo Women employed there—Museum—Academy for Native Artists—Cigarrillos—Igorroté—Our Excursion into the Interior—Description of a Casco—Laguna de Bayo—Binan—Hospitality of the Mestizos—Flying Foxes—Rice Fields—Los Banos—Lake of Makilign—Night at Calamba—Village of Tenauan—Cock Fight . . . 31

CHAPTER III.

An Accident—Lonely Walk to Laguna de Taal—Perplexities—The Friend in Need—Sugar Factory—Night's Lodging—Tagalo Predilection for Semi-hatched Eggs—Sail on the Lake—Island of Taal—Description of Volcano—Village of Talassig—Ruins of a Church—Return to Shore—Journey back in a Buffalo Cart—Sleep at Tanauan—Arrive at Binan—Proceed Next Day to Manilla—Signor C.—— kindly removed all our Things from the Hotel, and wishes us to stay till we leave—Delightful Fortnight—Departure from Manilla . . 77

CHAPTER IV.

The Happy Valley at Hong Kong—Go to Macao—"Breakers ahead"—Origin of the Name of Macao—Reason for the Fall of the Place—The Pagoda—A Woman trying her Fortune—Mode of doing so—Camoën's Garden—Monument of the Bard—Epitome of his Life 105

CHAPTER V.

Forts—Ruins of the Jesuit Church and College—A Chinaman's Disappointment—Angling near the Green Island—Murder of Governor Amarals—Arrest of a Young English Missionary—Return to Hong Kong—Voyage to Shanghae . . 121

CHAPTER VI.

Description of Shanghae—The European Settlements—Coolies carrying Parcels—Pigeon English—Chinese Anecdotes—Boats—Manner of Burying the Dead—The Troops—Attack on the North Gate—Chin-chilling the Ground—Mode of

CONTENTS. xi

Building—Wall of the City—Filthy Sights—Walk through Shanghae — Restaurants — Marriage Ceremonies — Joss Houses 133

CHAPTER VII.

Chinese Women—Men—Long Tails—Punishment of the Cangue—Superstition—Flavour of Tea—Growth of the Plant—Remarks on Green Tea—Population of China, and Food of the Poorer Classes—Bird's-Nest Soup—Gelatinous Food—The Form of Salutation—Ceremony of Kow-Tow—Chinese Idea of Geography—The Emperor's Hint—The Tae-pings, or Rebels—Taking of Kahding—Cruelty of the Rebels—Palanquins—Sad Accident to a Young Officer—Chinese Conveyance—" Baby Towers "—Infanticide—Birth of a Daughter no Cause of Rejoicing 159

CHAPTER VIII.

Set Sail for Japan—Anecdotes on Board—Vessel becalmed—Weary Time—Cape Gotto in sight at last—Entrance to Nagasaki Harbour—Lovely Scenery—Pappenberg—Its Dismal Tale—Peculiar Sail—Slight Clothing of the Men—Description of Dress of Officials—The Hara Kari—Our Home—Flowers—Streets of Nagasaki—Visit to the Tea-Firing Establishment—Silk-Mercers—Lacquer Ware—Porcelain—Picnic to Nazumisima 177

CHAPTER IX.

General View of Nagasaki Harbour—The Iron Foundry—Temple—Priests—Their Dress—Japanese Curiosity—" Man's Tail "

—Japanese Women—Their Dress—Men's Mode of wearing Hair—Immorality—Visit to a Yacoonin's—Wife's Devotion—Japanese Ladies come to see us—Their Pocket-Handkerchiefs—Articles of Domestic Use—A Family Meal—Ink Horn—Pillow—Overshoe—Straw Sandals, &c.—Japanese Mode of punishing those who offend Europeans—A Funeral Procession The Signal Hill—Excursion to Tookits . , . 199

CHAPTER X.

Passage to Yokohama—" Ship no walkee "—We enter the Inland Sea—Beautiful Nights—Bay of Yeddo—Fusiyama—Town of Yokohama—Fires in the Native Part—Country about—Excursion to Kama-Kura and beyond—Ride—Our Footmen—Tattooing—Singular Temple—Story attached to it—Huge Bell—Difficulty in discovering Diebutzu—Found at last—Return to Kanagawa—Ladies' Hair-Dressing going on—Description of Implements used—Mirrors . . . 223

CHAPTER XI.

Our Return to Yokohama—Salt Drying and Boiling—Weasels and Rats—Japanese Houses—Want of Chimney—Sliding Doors and Windows—Fire-Houses—Fans—Earthquakes—Japanese Accompaniments to a Gift—Kanagawa—The Norimons—Japanese mode of Announcing the Names of their Visitors—Our Disappointment—We Leave Yokohama—Bad Weather—Contretemps—Fortunate Escape in the Straits of Simonosaki—Straits of Herado—Arrival at Nagasaki—Reception there—Visit to a Merchant's House—Cool Request of his Wife—Yacoonin's Impression of his own Musical Talents—Japanese Theatre—Kind Offer 251

CHAPTER XII.

Return to Shanghae—Voyage to Hong Kong—Typhoon—We put in at Amoy—Go Ashore there—Tame Chinese Tiger—Dismasted Ships entering the Port—Death of a Chinaman on Board—Singular Request of his Friends—Safe Arrival at Victoria—Typhoon there—Another Peep at Macao—We go to Canton—Pagodas—Bodies Floating down the Stream—Intense Heat—Joss-House—Singular Monument for an English Sailor—Illuminated Boats on the River—Return to Victoria—Feast of Lanterns—Curious Substitute for Machinery 281

CHAPTER I.

LEAVE SINGAPORE FOR HONG KONG—LIFE ON BOARD—ARRIVE AT VICTORIA—ASCEND THE PEAK—GO TO MANILLA—WRETCHED THREE DAYS' VOYAGE—FILTHY STEAMER—MANILLA BAY—CUSTOM-HOUSE—HOTEL—A DRIVE TO HEAR THE BAND—FIRES—LANDLADY'S SUGGESTIONS AS TO THE CAUSE OF THEM—BIGOTRY OF THE INHABITANTS—TAXES—DESCRIPTION OF THE TOWN—STATUE OF THE QUEEN—ORIGIN OF THE NAME OF LUZON—DESCRIPTION OF A NATIVE WOMAN—BARRACKS AND PRISON—USES OF THE BAMBOO—BUFFALOES VERY NUMEROUS—MANGOES—CHOCOLATE.

CHAPTER I.

MARCH 2, Sunday, 1862.—We left Singapore for Hong Kong. Our boat, the *Thunder*, an opium clipper, commanded by an able captain, was a fast one, and for two days we cut through the great deep at a very quick rate. The passengers were all agreeable, and as the wife of the captain accompanied her husband, we spent many pleasant hours in her cheerful cabin on deck.

Captain and Mrs. —— are real canny Scotch folk, and it was no fault of theirs if the passengers were not comfortable. We passed our time in the regular steam-boat fashion, eating, drinking, laughing, singing, and walking the same prescribed limit each day, with the usual results at night, a sigh and a groan as we left the cool deck, where the night dews were falling fast, and turned into our close quarters below, to see, by the light of the oil lamp, the cockroaches cutting capers over our narrow couch, and diving under the pillow and into our shoes by way of concealment. For the latter articles these horrid insects have a decided predilection, and it is by no means an uncommon occurrence to find the leather in great part eaten away over night. I always provide myself with a large stock of camphor, which certainly has the effect in a great degree of banishing them, as they dislike the smell, and, after the first night or two, fly your cabin, as human beings would do a plague-stricken house. I must confess the *Thunder* had fewer cockroaches than most vessels in these warm regions; but even in her I, who have a singular aversion to these insects, was honoured by the sight of them on many occasions.

Well, thus we sped, and on we went merrily and cheerily, the sun rising brightly and setting in all his eastern glory, till Tuesday morning, when a change came over the "spirit of our dreams." The wind over night had risen, and the China sea, rarely a very tranquil one, now boiled as though Neptune had suddenly become furious, and, like a frantic steed, sought to unseat its rider; for we tossed, rolled, and pitched, till every moveable article had changed its place over and over again, and the woe-begone faces of some of our *compagnons de voyage* contrasted sadly with the bright eyes and beaming smiles of the previous day.

As I am in general a good sailor, I had leisure to observe and compassionate the miserable state of the others, and at the same time could philosophize a little on the cause of their sufferings. After five days of this commotion, the wind began to abate and the sea to grow calmer. This you might perceive from a glance at the invalids, whose faces proved capital weather-glasses, for the corners of their mouths began to be drawn up and their heavy eye-lids to rise.

On Monday morning, about five, we caught sight of land, and about half-past six were just off the Lema Islands, which consist of a few barren and uninhabited rocks, abounding in caves and holes, the occasional retreat of pirates, numbers of whom infest these seas. Here we stayed for about eight hours, "laying to," our sails unfurled, but our engines dormant; waiting to give the agents in Hong Kong every advantage of the Calcutta news concerning the market price of opium, for which purpose the purser had been despatched in a boat immediately on our stopping, the *Thunder* being a private boat, and only carrying a few passengers as a convenience. Of course we all rushed on deck to feast our eyes with a sight of something in the shape of land; and though we found nothing very attractive in the bare peaks and rocks, one of which, rising in two long pillars from one base, goes by the name of " The Ass's Ears," yet we derived a certain degree of satisfaction from the view, and had a fresh topic for conversation.

At half-past two we started anew, and passed through the Taitami Channel, meeting a number of fishing boats on our way. These are formed something in the shape of a Belgian sabot, turning up at each end. We very nearly ran down one in our rapid course. I was in Mrs. ———'s cabin at the time the " gude-wife" was tempting her "gude-mon" with some delicious soup; for this was a busy day for Captain ———, who, when duty was in the way, never thought of meals, and would most likely have gone all day without one, had not his true helpmate and faithful companion been ever at hand to watch and to minister.

Captain —— had just finished and reached the cabin door, when he espied the hazardous position of the fishing craft, which had escaped notice before. Immediately giving orders to " stop," the men were rescued from their perilous position; and the boat passed so near our lee-bow, that the voice of the superior could be clearly distinguished, as he spoke in no mild terms to the awkward steersman, who took his scolding in a very philosophic manner, which I accounted for by the supposition that it required a more than ordinary matter to disturb the equanimity of a cool Chinaman.

We passed a number of small islands, all more or less barren and rocky. As we appproached the Island of Hong Kong we saw Stanley Barracks, but quickly lost sight of them, as the Island of Lama, a long, uninhabited island, in the possession of the British, intercepted our view, leaving only the peaks of Hong Kong visible, amidst which that named Victoria stood conspicuous. Passing this, and leaving the Islands of Lantao, Chung, &c., to our left, we soon came in full view of the town of Hong Kong, with its tiers of streets and houses, many of the latter new, and some unfinished. I was agreeably surprised at the pleasing aspect the town presented, for I had heard much of its barren situation, but nothing of its beauty. It is situated at the foot of the highest peak, called Victoria Peak, and many of the country seats of the influential merchants are built quite in elevated positions, forming delightful retreats in the warm weather. One of the most charming of these belongs to our kind host, Mr. R., a Portuguese gentleman, who, with his wife and family, gave us a most hospitable reception. He was the first who devised the idea of building high up on the rock, from which the governor bestowed upon him the appellation of the "Pioneer," as others have since followed his example.

By five o'clock we landed, and I, entering one of the palanquins (my husband walking with our friend by the side), was quickly conveyed, by two stout-looking Chinamen, to our destination. These palanquins are entirely different from those in Calcutta. They consist of a chair, made of bamboo, with a species of awning or cover, and one in front to put down in case of rain. The whole is supported on two strong bamboo poles, which are brought near together at the extremities, allowing a space for the bearer's head, so that the two ends rest on each shoulder. To enter one of these, the first Chinaman raises the two front portions of the poles, you dive your head below, and, when within the two, he lets it rest, and you take your seat.

Like Malta, the streets of Hong Kong are, for the most part, a continual ascent and descent—that is to say, all which conduct to those running in tiers up the hill. The shops of ivory wares, &c., &c., are very conspicuous, and look most tempting.

As we arrived in the cooler weather, we were easily able to mount the Peak, a pleasant little excursion, which we made on the Wednesday following — nothing to those who have trod the mountains of Switzerland or Savoy, who have ascended, on foot, to Montanvert, in Chamouni, and, traversing the Mer de Glace, arrived at that beautiful oasis, in a desert of snow, called the "Jardin," or who have climbed the Pyramid in Egypt, and gazed from its summit on the vast plain of sand and the ugly Sphinx beneath, but, nevertheless, a pleasant little excursion. It takes about an hour to ascend leisurely, and a little more than half that time to descend, for the road is admirably kept, and the view from the top amply rewards the exertion. The harbour of Hong Kong, with its numerous barques, brigs, steamers, and small boats, forms a pleasing sight; and the governor's house, with the new pleasure-garden in front, looks very pretty. Behind the town, as you ascend, you can see, between an opening in the rocks, the race-ground, a space of land called the Happy Valley, apparently perfectly level, and kept in beautiful order. Near the summit is situated the Sanatorium, a hospital to which invalids, both civil and military, resort. On the top is the watch-house, or observatory, a round tower with a vane at the roof. The flag-staff is placed a few feet lower down, on which are hoisted the signals for each vessel making its way into port.

We returned by the other side, and thus caught a glimpse of the sea beyond the harbour; and here the view is most lovely, only requiring a little more verdure to make it enchanting. Unfortunately, but few trees grow here, on account of the winds; and those which do manage to eke out a feeble existence, look stunted and weak, as though, could they speak, they would say, "What pleasure to us is life amid these barren rocks?"

The sun was nearly setting as we reached the edge of the cliff on which Mr. R's. house is situated, and as the water was calm and undisturbed, save for the ripple against the sides of the rock, the scene was truly grand, diversified as it was by so many rocky islands, some small, others large, and all possessing numerous creeks and tiny bays, in the waters of which the overhanging rocks appeared beautifully reflected, the little white sails of the boats in the distance, seemingly without any boat beneath, looking like birds borne on by the slight movement of the waters.

We left this pleasing scene, to return to one of commotion and bustle; for we had to pack up and arrange our little matters in order to start for Manilla by the boat which was to leave next morning. So, bidding adieu to quiet and tranquillity, we once more set ourselves to work, and next morning, by half-past seven, were on board the steamship *P*——, bound for Manilla. Here we found none of the *Thunder* comforts. The boat was manned by Spanish sailors, and was a kind of semi man-of-war. We found the officers very attentive and kind, but the vessel awfully dirty, and the food very greasy. We encountered very unpleasant weather, and spent a wretched time; for our baby was sick as well as ourselves, and the China boy, whom we had engaged in preference to a woman—on hearing he was an excellent sailor—was literally useless. To add to all our discomforts, the boat was a clumsily-built one, little suited to these seas, and tossed and rolled just as a tub would have done. Fortunately we made a pretty quick passage, and arrived an hour or two within three days. The heat during the last twenty-four hours had become intense, and the air close and stifling.

About half-past eight on Sunday we entered the little boat which was to convey us to shore, happy in the thought of speedily arriving there; but, alas! short-sighted mortals! after a weary pull of an hour, we only reached the end of a long pier, which two men mounted, and then began towing us along. The boat was a neat, clean specimen of Manilla handicraft, being scooped out of one entire large trunk of teak wood, with a neatly-constructed awning of matting, and a nice sort of frame-work for our feet to rest on, so that, in case the water came in, we could not get wet. The oars were of the paddle species, with handles at the end like those of a spade. The men looked clean and hardy, with features very much of the Malay type.

Arrived at the end of the pier, the men re-entered the boat, and rowed us to the opposite side, where a custom-house officer entered. As we had but few things, we never dreamt of much detention, more especially as our passport had been already examined by the officer who came on board for that purpose. So we patiently endured the trouble of waiting to take in this man, then rowing back to the other side, and disembarking all our luggage. But lo and behold! it appeared we had not half done yet. The things had to be left while we proceeded to another part to get a pass for them— they alleging as an excuse that it was Sunday; but I strongly suspect that to this suspicious government all days are alike for giving trouble to foreigners.

Well, finally, the things were passed, and weary with the heat and glare—for it was near eleven before all was arranged—we entered the hotel of Madame du Bosse, delighted with the prospect of rest and quietness.

In the evening, we took a drive to the Calçada, whither numbers of carriages were whirling—the gay world of Manilla, decked out in colours bright, radiant, and numerous as those of the rainbow. Four native military bands had taken up their stations near each other when we arrived, and, at the moment our vehicle drew up, one was playing some sweet low air in a manner very well worthy of commendation. As one band ceased another commenced, so the intervals between each melody were very short. Some ladies, I perceived, wore the mantilla, with its graceful folds falling over their shoulders, but these were few in number, for the generality wear neither bonnet nor hat for the evening promenade, but, like the Dutch ladies in Java, prefer thoroughly to enjoy the fresh air.

The Manilla ponies reminded us much of the Javanese. Like them they are very strong, but not of a large size, and run at a rapid rate, some of them having a most agreeable ambling trot.

En route we saw the ruins of several houses which had been destroyed by fire, and on speaking with our landlady, she informed us that this month (March) is proverbially known as the month for this scourge. On my asking the reason, she replied she knew not, but her own opinion was, that this being the grand festal month of the whole year, a number of the natives, male and female, endeavour to array themselves as finely as possible. Many, being too poor to afford the peña, embroidered handkerchiefs, shirts, jewels, &c., &c., set fire to dwellings, or employ others to do so, in order that in the general confusion they may steal whatever valuables they can lay hands on. A gentleman subsequently gave me another version of the cause of these incendiary proceedings. "Whenever," he observed, "these fires occur there is sure to be a quantity of bamboo on the hands of the wood-merchants, for which they can get little or nothing, owing to there being no demand. The houses are generally burnt to the ground, for, being constructed principally or entirely of bamboo and attap, it is difficult to arrest the progress of the flames. The day after the conflagration, the quantity of bamboo for which a merchant could only get twenty-five cents, is worth fully two dollars." Which of these two statements is to be regarded as the true explanation of the fact in question, I cannot say; but all must agree that, as there is never a fire without a cause, there may be some probability in both of them.

The people in Manilla are awfully bigoted, more priest-ridden, *if possible*, than in Spain itself, and, consequently, far behind in every kind of industrial or intellectual pursuit. Influenced by the priests, they evince a marked dislike to anything in the shape of innovations. No Protestant missionary is allowed to set foot in one of the Philippines, nor, if known, is a Protestant Bible suffered to enter; in proof of which, a gentleman told me he passed his through the custom-house by putting it under his hat.

About three years ago a miraculous performance took place at one of the churches. The wounds of a figure representing our Saviour began to run copiously with blood; and very soon the credulous inhabitants crowded in dense masses to the church where the spectacle was exhibiting, to witness the *miracle*. Money poured in from all sides, and the joy of the officiating priests at the success of their scheme was extreme—when "a change came over the spirit of their dream." The more enlightened, who saw through this wicked subterfuge, determined to expose the deception. The image was accordingly examined, and found to contain tubes, through which the red liquid was pumped up from below.

Almost all the inhabitants of the island of Luzon are Christian, or, at least, nominally so; and in nearly every village is a church, with one or two officiating priests, whose influence is extraordinarily great. A Roman Catholic priest, in his work called "Recollections of a Journey through Tartary, Thibet, and China," in alluding to the conversion of the natives, says:

"It seems to us that the beauty of the Roman Catholic ceremonies must act powerfully on a people so fond of all that relates to external worship." *

A plain admission of the influence, on the minds of a superstitious people, of the numerous images and extravagantly gaudy processions, &c., &c.,

* Translation of Mons. Huc's work.

by which the Roman Catholics so powerfully impress the imaginations of the ignorant; while our simpler and purer forms often fail, through that very simplicity which is their greatest beauty, in rousing their devotion—reminding one of the narrow way, which has no gaudy flowers to attract those drawn only by the imagination, and not through the heart.

The heat in the Philippines is intense during the months of August, September, October, and November; but during the rainy season the atmosphere is cool, the rain falling in torrents, though rarely sufficiently heavy to destroy the slight bamboo houses of the natives.

All the inhabitants of the Philippines pay a tax to the Spanish Government, from the age of sixteen, if orphans, and twenty, should both parents be alive. This ceases entirely at sixty. Each mestizo, or half-caste, pays fifteen reals—about one dollar and a half—being about half-a-dollar more than every native; whilst the poor Chinamen, of whom there are fully ten thousand in the whole of Luzon, are obliged to give up three dollars each. The latter seem universally disliked and laughed at. Though I do not admire many traits in a Chinaman's character and disposition, I cannot but think this most unjust, for they are a hardworking, industrious people, and very persevering; emigrating to all European settlements in the East, and ekeing out an existence where many would starve, in every branch of trade completely superseding the natives, who are more inactive and less self-denying. This of course is prejudicial to the interest of the inhabitants, and therefore the Chinese in Java and Manilla are so hardly dealt with, and prove such unwelcome intruders.

As nearly all the inhabitants of Luzon are Christians, and but few of the Chinese, they find it very difficult to obtain wives—the Roman Catholic priests positively refusing to marry any Christian to an infidel; and, as the Chinese women scarcely ever leave their own country, the consequence is that their lives are but too frequently frightfully immoral.

There are about two thousand, in all, of the Philippine Islands, only five or six hundred of them being of any size or importance. Luzon, the largest, contains seventeen provinces, and has for its capital Manilla, situated on the Bay of Manilla, which is said to be thirty leagues in circumference. The island is about four hundred miles in length, and two hundred broad, being narrower towards the south than the north. The position of Manilla is remarkably good, the sea on one side, and the river on the other, with ditches —well fortified on the land between. Manilla is the name given to that part of the town within the walls of Fort St. Iago. The rest of it is called, by the Spaniards, "Estras Muros," for the greater number of the houses are now outside the walls.

The fort is quadrangular in shape, and surrounded by an outer wall and fosse. There are six gates, and these are regularly closed at an hour past midnight. Gentlemen and ladies frequenting late balls or parties, and requiring entrance or exit after the usual hour, are obliged to obtain a permit from the Captain of the guard.

There are a number of squares; the principal one has the Cathedral, a heavy-looking building, on the south side, and the Governor's palace on the west; the custom-house and town-hall are also situated inside the fort, and a military as well as a public hospital.

To the south, beyond the walls, is the Calçada, of which I have before spoken. To arrive at this place from the fort you must cross Ponte Grande, and traverse a fine broad road, lined on either side by trees. They are very particular at the time of the evening promenade, placing mounted police, equipped very much like the French gendarmes, to prevent any carriage from going into the centre of the road, and to see that the regular sides for going and returning are kept, a heavy fine being imposed on any offender against the rules, which, although rather strict, I must admit, prevent much confusion and many accidents.

The new theatre stands to the right of Ponte Grande, a short distance from the pretty barracks facing the river, and near the new gardens, which now occupy a site where, a few years back, nothing was to be seen but a marshy field.

In front of the theatre is placed the statue of Queen Isabel the Second of Spain; the pedestal, which is of dark Romblon marble, and cost five thousand dollars, bears the following inscription in Spanish :—" El Ayuntamiento de Manila, en nombre de los habitantes de Filipinas, a sa Dona Isabel II.," on the front. On the right hand side are these words: " Se proyecto en 1854;" and on the left, " Se inauguró en 1860." At the back, in an "escudo," there is a lion rampant, bearing a sword. This statue was made by a distinguished sculptor, named D. Ponciano Ponzano, at a cost of ten thousand dollars, and was sent from Cadiz in the Spanish vessel *Alavasa*. There is a statue to the memory of Magellan on the left side of Ponte Grande.

It is stated that when Magellan's party first landed on the island of Luzon, they saw a woman pounding rice in the manner followed by the natives to this day—that is, in a mortar formed by scooping out a large hole in the trunk of a tree, about two or three feet high. On their making signs of wishing to know what she was doing, she held up the large piece of wood which acted as a pestle, and called out "Looson," which is the term used by the natives for the whole implement. From this circumstance the Spaniards called the island Luçon.

We saw a picture of this scene by a native artist, who had taken considerable artistic licence in painting it. As far as dress and attitude were concerned, the figure was such a one as is frequently seen in Manilla, and more frequently still in its environs, and near the Lagunas; but certainly better-looking, fairer, and taller than any Tagalo we saw during our stay in the isle. As it is truly said, however, that there is no rule with-

out an exception, the elegant female Aguador
may have been as beautiful as she is represented
by the painter whose work we had the good
fortune to see.

The upper portion of female dress in Luzon
consists of a short jacket, which is very loose
and cool, being of a light texture. The colour
generally worn is dark blue, which is a favourite
among the poorer people, probably from the
fact of their being able to wear it longer, and
so avoid the constant washing required by a
light-coloured material. The skirt, or "syab,"
as it is called, is very long, and worn tied round
the waist. As they wear no under-garments,
this simple dress is admirably adapted for a
climate where frequently the temperature varies
from 85° to 100° Fahrenheit.

Like the Indian women, the females of Manilla are accustomed from childhood to carry
heavy weights; and the perfect ease with which
they walk with their jars balanced on their
heads is really wonderful. They are often seen
carrying in their right hand a portion of a plantain leaf, which they will probably use as a plate
at their next meal; and they generally have the

forethought to put some into the water in the jar, to prevent it becoming tepid, a practice common amongst all natives of the East.

The neckerchief usually worn is coloured. Few in the humbler "station of life" wear white, except on Sundays, when they obtain a peña if possible, with as much embroidery on it as they can afford to pay for. Occasionally a female is seen very quietly dressed, as far as her skirt is concerned, but they generally choose the gaudiest colours and "*loudest*" patterns. A small square article which they wear suspended from their necks both day and night, is a charm, and is supposed to keep off evil spirits. They buy these, or are presented with them by the priest of the *pueblo*, or village, who sprinkles them with holy water, to increase their magic effect. A picture, meant to represent Christ, the Virgin and Child, or some particular saint, is either worked or sketched upon this bit of red cloth.

During our day in Manilla, my husband visited the prison and barracks, and from the notes he there made I extract the following:

"April 3rd.—Went with Major T—— to the barracks of the 5th regiment, situated about a mile and a half from Manilla. It consists of two buildings divided by the main road. The one on the left hand side was formerly the officers' quarters, and is now converted into common barracks for the men, their superiors preferring a life nearer town. I found the rooms for the men very clean and neat; at the door of the division for each company a soldier was stationed, whose business it was to acquaint the men inside with the approach of any officer. As we left I observed in the court-yard that the native troops were undergoing inspection, and very neat and orderly they looked; much superior in stature and bearing to the Javanese soldiers under the Dutch Government. We next went to the Presidio, or prison, where I was introduced to the Governor. In the store-room I saw some link chains for the prisoners, weighing from four up to ten pounds. I observed that all was kept in a model way as to cleanliness, from the kitchen to the prisons. The bed-rooms consist of two oblong rooms, running at right angles; the men sleep on a platform raised about two feet from the ground, slightly inclined, with a block of wood for a pillow—perhaps you may say a suitable one for their hardened hearts, to cause reflection, and, we'll hope, repentance.

"All the prisoners are chained together in pairs, so that the actions of one must influence those of the other. At the foot of each man's couch poles are placed about ten feet apart, upon which the jailor suspends their chains, so that the men on guard are immediately aware of their slightest movement. They are fed very well; their meals regulated as follows:—At six A.M. they have a large tin can of coffee and a similar sized one of rice; at eight, rice and fish; twelve, rice and meat; and, finally, for the evening, at six, rice and meat again.

"If any prisoner makes his escape, and is retaken, he has the letter F affixed to his back, but if caught in the act of trying to escape he has only C F.

"Those who try to avoid labour by purposely cutting and maiming themselves, have a large monkey, made of red cloth, patched on the back of their dress; monkey, in the Tagalo language, is called "chongo," and is the most contemptuous epithet you can bestow on a native of these parts—being as repugnant to his feelings as the term "swar," or pig, is to a Mussulman of India.

I saw a number with this mark, which, but for the explanation, would have puzzled me.

"I observe that here, as in India, Java, and the Straits, the bamboo serves, at least, a hundred purposes. As a young plant it is eaten, stewed, or pickled; whilst the old tree becomes vessels for water, water-pipes, &c., &c.

"Baffaloes are very numerous in this country, and great use is made of them. We drank buffalo milk, I believe, the whole time we were in the island. It is very sweet, and, I was told, very nutritious, but I did not like the flavour so well as that of cow's milk.

"Fortunately we were here during the mango season, and were able to feast upon this most delicious fruit. We also enjoyed the chocolate very much, preferring it, however, thinner than it is generally liked here."

CHAPTER II.

THE CATHEDRAL—CURIOUS PICTURES—OLD LEGEND OF SAINT CHRISTOPHER—VISIT TO THE CEMETERY—TALES—CIGAR MANUFACTORY—DESCRIPTION OF TAGALO WOMEN EMPLOYED THERE—MUSEUM—ACADEMY FOR NATIVE ARTISTS—CIGARRILLOS—IGORROTÉ—OUR EXCURSION INTO THE INTERIOR—DESCRIPTION OF A CASCO—LAGUNA DE BAYO—BINAN—HOSPITALITY OF THE MESTIZOS—FLYING FOXES—RICE FIELDS—LOS BANOS—LAKE OF MAKILIGN—NIGHT AT CALAMBA—VILLAGE OF TENAUAN—COCK FIGHT.

CHAPTER II.

THE exterior of the Cathedral is very ordinary and heavy, as are all the churches and public buildings.

On entering, the principal altar presents a most gorgeous spectacle, being apparently one mass of silver; but, on closer examination, we found the only portion that was really so was a thin plating which made a dazzling effect. In a frame above are a number of figures symbolical of our Saviour's Crucifixion—the cross, dice, ladder, spears, and garments, &c., &c.—but at a first glance they all looked like hieroglyphics on a freemason's apron.

There are numbers of small chapels, and a very fine dome; but beyond this nothing struck us much, except two very curious pictures. In one the Virgin Mary was represented standing on a tree in an arbour, with a priest, surrounded by Europeans on one side, and a number of natives on the other—all faces presenting an awe-struck, wondering expression. The inscription below informed us that this was a miraculous appearance of the Virgin in this island, some hundred years ago, or more. Singular to relate, in the distance a steamer is seen on the sea, smoking and puffing. We thought this accorded strangely with the date—unless, indeed, its appearance there might be accounted for as the effect of another miracle!

The other picture represented a huge-looking man bearing a little child on his shoulders. Apparently he is sinking from fatigue, and clings for support to a tree in the middle of the river he is crossing. This is the Roman Catholic saint, St. Christopher; and the legend connected with the picture I cannot better describe than by quoting that pretty little poem by the author of "John Halifax, Gentleman."

THE LEGEND OF ST. CHRISTOPHER.

"Carry me across!"
The Syrian heard, rose up, and braced
  His huge limbs to the accustomed toil!
"My child, see how the waters boil!
The night-black heavens look angry-faced;
  But life is little loss.

"I'll carry thee with joy,
If needs be, safe as nestling dove;
 For o'er this stream I pilgrims bring,
 In service to one Christ, a King,
Whom I have never seen, yet love."
 "I thank thee," said the boy.

 Cheerful, Arprobus took
The burthen on his shoulders great,
 And stepped into the waves once more;
 When, lo! they leaping rise and roar,
And 'neath the little child's light weight
 The tottering giant shook.

 "Who art thou?" cried he, wild
Struggling in middle of the ford.
 "Boy as thou look'st, it seems to me
 The whole world's load I bear in thee;
Yet"—"For the sake of Christ, the Lord,
 Carry me," said the child.

 No more Arprobus swerved,
But gained the further bank, and then
 A voice cried, "Hence Christopheros be!
 For carrying, thou hast carried Me,
The King of angels and of men,
 The Master thou hast served."

 And in the moonlight blue,
The saint saw, not the wandering boy,
 But Him who walked upon the sea,

And o'er the plains of Galilee,
'Till, filled with mystic, awful joy,
His dear Lord Christ he knew.

.   .   .

Oh! little is all loss,
And brief the space 'twixt shore and shore.
If Thou, Lord Jesus, on us lay,
Through the deep waters of our way,
The burthen that Christopheros bore—
To carry Thee across.

We went one day to St. Anna, a small village about two miles distant, by the St. Miguel road, where, to the left, we saw a new hospital in course of erection. Leaving this road we turned to the right and entered that called Mercelingo, where, crossing a small bridge over the little stream of Balété, a charming view is obtained of the distant high hills of St. Matéo and Anitipolo. On our return we visited the cemetery, situated about a mile and a half from town; a place of singular construction, through which one cannot walk without experiencing a thrill of horror. It is formed in a double circle, with a church at the end of the centre walk. Between the outer and inner circle there is a space of ground left for the poor, who are interred uncoffined, quicklime being strewn over the corpse to hasten decomposition. In the thick solid walls are three parallel rows of horizontal recesses, at short intervals from each other, capable of admitting a good-sized coffin. Here are deposited the bodies of those whose relatives are able to pay sixteen dollars (about three pounds twelve shillings). The entrance is then bricked up, and a plate fixed outside, stating the name, age, profession, &c., of the lonely occupant, who is left undisturbed for the space of three years, at the expiration of which time, should the relatives or friends desire it, they make the necessary arrangements, and the bones of the deceased are collected and buried in one of the churches. The bodies not thus removed are taken from the coffin and thrown into a species of Golgotha attached to the cemetery, into which you look from a high terrace, or walk, on the wall, reached by means of a long flight of steps not far from the church. The sight is sad enough, but it is more melancholy still to witness the perfect indifference, nay, more, even the jocular manner of the guides, as, with a smile, they point out to you these last relics of humanity, all indiscriminately heaped up together, and fast dissolving away by means of the lime thrown in from time to time.

Near this place are two crescent-shaped cemeteries, attached, as far as I can recollect, to the large circle on one side, and to the receptacle for bones on the other. These are for little children, and are arranged on the same principle as the others.

Within the space enclosed by the interior wall is a large plot of ground, likewise for the poor, studded with shady trees. Round the inner side of each circle there is a walk, where you can inspect the names of the departed; and not unfrequently you see a hole just broken into, or a coffin from which the bones have been taken out, partially re-filled by cockroaches and other insects, doubtless attracted there by the putrescent effluvia.

There are many stories related of this place. The following were recounted to me as perfectly true:

About five years ago a captain in the Navy made a bet with his comrades that he would go and sleep in the cemetery. Accordingly he set out alone, and, having provided himself with an ample supply of alcoholic liquor, he thought by imbibing spirits to drive spirits away. With a bold step he entered, and, walking into the inner circle, mounted the wall, on which seating himself, he placed the bottle to his lips; but, alas for the shortsightedness of human nature! instead of increasing his courage, the more he drank the more nervous he became, till at last, fancy conjuring up all kinds of spectres, he rose hastily, believing himself pursued by some object of terror. He attempted to quit his perilous position, but, his legs being very unsteady, he approached too near the edge of the parapet, missed his footing, and fell to the ground below, where he was picked up dead the following morning.

A young priest, once wishing to show his courage, and the contemptuous light in which he regarded all superstitious notions, laid a considerable wager that he would walk to the cemetery in the dead of night, and hammer a nail into a certain part of the inner wall. Leaving the town at the stated time, he proceeded straight to the place, and arrived there, perfectly satisfied of his ability to perform the lonely task he had imposed upon himself. Advancing into the inner circle, he planted a small ladder, with which he was provided, against the wall, and before proceeding further, looked leisurely around. The moon was shining in full beauty, and her rays, tipping the leaves of all the trees on one side of the circle, shed a subdued light on every object immediately around our adventurer, leaving the other side of this portion of the cemetery, into which the moon's rays could not penetrate, in perfect shade. Spite of every wish to the contrary, the poor priest could not but feel a kind of undefined dread at the awful stillness, and, as he slowly ascended the ladder, his knees began perceptibly to tremble. Determined, however, to execute his purpose, he fixed the nail and commenced hammering loudly—his perturbed spirit deriving comfort from the reverberating sounds thus created. Quite reassured when this work was finished, he turned in order to descend, when, putting his foot out to place it on the ladder, he felt his cape pulled from behind. Too terrified to try and ascertain the cause, he made several attempts to disengage himself, but the more he pulled, the faster he seemed to be held; until at last, exhausted with the efforts he had made, he remained passive from terror. The whole cemetery seemed whirling around him. The coffins appeared to be leaving their narrow cells, and their lids bursting open, he fancied he saw the ghastly inmates grinning at him. In vain he tried to cry out, his tongue refused to frame a single word; and thus, paralysed by fear, his senses entirely forsook him, and he fell to the ground below, where he remained in a state of unconsciousness until discovered by a friend many hours after, who, fearing something had happened, came, accompanied by others, to search for him. He slowly recovered his senses, but spoke little, although the remembrance of all that had happened remained impressed by terror on his mind. Notwithstanding his friends pointed out to him the rent in his cape, which, having caught on the nail when he turned round, was torn as he fell from the ladder, he smiled incredulously, and gradually sank, till he died in the full belief that what he had witnessed was a punishment for his daring to boast on such a subject.

On another occasion a priest died and was interred here. The night after his burial some people who were about heard strange noises, apparently issuing from his tomb. They immediately communicated this to the priest who lived in the premises opposite; but regarding their fears as idle superstition, he bade them *va con Dios*, and not repeat such nonsense again. They accordingly retired, but the representations made by them in the town the next day caused an immediate investigation. The coffin of the priest was opened, when, to the horror of all present, he was found to have changed his position, having been entombed whilst in a trance, and it was evident that he had died while biting his own arm in the agonies of suffocation.

A young lady's body was found after three years interment fresh as the day she was buried. This was looked upon by the people of the Philippines as a miracle, though we all well know it must have been the result of some idiosyncrasy in the constitution, as similar cases have occurred in Europe, though they are very rare.

Soon after our arrival in Manilla, Signor C. brought his son, and his daughter, Signora O., to visit us, and they kindly took us to the cigar manufactory, which interested us greatly. The building is very extensive, covering six acres, in a quarter of the town called Binondo, and was erected about the year 1782. The tobacco seed was brought first in 1780 from Mexico, and, on being planted, flourished so well that they then determined to commence the manufacture of cigars. They employ in this establishment ten thousand women,* and three hundred men, the wages of each being thirty cents per day. As they have no machinery, all is done by manual labour; and to us, so used to the former in Europe, the latter process seemed slow. The building contains four galleries, each being divided into two or three compartments. You walk down the middle of these galleries, where, at long low tables on each side, the women work, seated upon mats placed on the ground. The noise is very deafening, for each female is provided with a stone, about the size of a large lemon, with which she beats the leaves continually, reminding one of cooks beating beefsteaks. When the "coat" is thus prepared, they put a quantity of small chopped up tobacco in the centre, a little gum on one edge, and then roll it very adroitly till it assumes the desired form, after which the small end is neatly

* This was named to me on the spot, and I made a note of it; but from my own observation, I should fancy the number to have been less.

tapered off. I regarded this mass of human beings attentively, and in no instance could discover one really pretty face. Some, indeed, had splendid dark eyes, but the rest of the face generally spoilt the effect this one beauty would have produced, the mouth, nose, and cheekbones being coarse and ill-formed. Many of them wore their hair loose, and in some it was so long that it reached the ground. This, with their small, delicately shaped hands, we admired very much, though I could not help contrasting their general appearance with the graceful beauty of the Indian women, whose fine large eyes and regular features so well accord with the perfect contour of their figures.

We next visited the department for men, and on entering found three hundred of them seated on benches before small tables. Although they had very little clothing on, they were evidently suffering from intense heat. These men are employed in the manufacture of a new cigar, Havannah shaped, which it is hoped will prove a very lucrative article of trade: they are called Beguéros. The leaf of which they are formed comes from Cagayan, a province in the north of the island of Luzon. It is considered quite a superior tobacco, and all they can obtain is devoted solely to making cigars.

Our kind friends now insisted on our accompanying them home, where we partook of an abundant breakfast, and then started afresh to see the "lions."

We first visited a sugar manufactory belonging to the widow of a Chinese Mandarin, who had turned Christian, married, settled, and died near Manilla.

The cane is not crushed here, but in the provinces, from whence it is conveyed, in lumps of raw sugar, to the Chinese merchants in Manilla, who place it in large jars, containing from about twenty to thirty pounds, spreading over it a layer of clay an inch or two thick.

In each of these earthen vessels is a hole, similar to that of a flower-pot, under which are placed smaller jars, into which the molasses drains itself, the sugar becoming whiter by degrees. The whole plan is very simple, but in Java it is conducted on a much better principle, and in a much cleaner way. There, instead of the earthen vessels below each jar, the whole floor is full of conduits, and the jars of sugar being placed over these, the whole quantity of molasses runs into a large reservoir at one end of the establishment.

The widow, a cheerful-looking body, born in the Philippines, but evidently of Chinese extraction, offered me a bouquet of oleanders, which flourish here abundantly, as in all warm climates. Then bringing an artificial rose, she bid me smell it. On complying with her request, I found she had scented it with otto of roses, which, doubtless, she meant as a great compliment. On looking round her house, as well as many others I afterwards visited, I did not marvel at the ease with which the Roman Catholic clergy convert these simple-minded people. Pictures, and images of saints, in all imaginable shapes and attitudes, in ivory, wood, gold, silver, and stone, adorn their walls and windows, whilst crosses abound at every turn, and dangle from the chains or rosaries that hang round every woman's neck. One cannot but draw his own inference from the fact that the more savage, the more wild and ignorant, a race of people are, the greater number of idols they worship, the less can they live by faith, and the more do they require external objects to remind them of Him whom they ought to adore in spirit and in truth.

The "Fabrica de Cigarrillos" is simple but curious. They have a machine, worked by two men, to cut papers into the required lengths for wrapping up the bundles of cigarrillos, and another to print upon them the government stamp, also employing two men. In the second story are seen men and boys, seated at tables, busily employed in manufacturing them. Each individual is supplied, by the superintendent, with a certain quantity of thin paper, out of which he tears strips the size of a cigaret, measured by his practised eye to a wonderful nicety. He then fills it with tobacco, chopped finely, by means of machinery, for a wonder! and rolls them tight, doubling each end with his thumb-nails, which are kept long on purpose, the right hand one being covered by a small leaden sheath, to strengthen and protect it.

A picture I saw of one of the aborigines of the Island of Luzon represented him as very lightly clad. With the exception of a bit of cloth round his loins, and the scarf hanging from his shoulder (which I am inclined to look upon as merely an artistic addition of the native limner), he may be said to have been *in puris naturalibus.*

A Spanish writer describes the Igorroté as dark in complexion, and, though small in stature, remarkably active. Their noses, he says, are broad and flat, the upper lip thick, and very large, the hair, which, with few exceptions, they wear short, dark and crisp, and perfectly free from any hair-dressing process; parting either down the middle, or at the side, being a fashion not yet introduced amongst these primitive islanders. Their bodies are tattoed with figures of snakes, frogs, lizards, and other ugly slimy reptiles (a species for which they have an especial admiration and veneration!), interspersed here and there with flowers and leaves, &c., &c.

Their food consists of fish, vegetables, and game, when they are fortunate enough, by means of their bows and arrows, to procure any of the latter; and as the mountains, where these people always live, generally abound in deer, wild boar, flying foxes, as well as forest pigeons and other birds, there is little chance of any sportsman amongst them returning home empty-handed from the chase.

The bow in hand, and quiver slung across the shoulder, may be considered almost to form a part of the man himself, for by day he is never seen without them, and by night they are placed close to his couch. The quiver, no doubt, contains many a poisoned barb, as well as arrows for ordinary purposes. The poison used is a preparation made out of the root and juice of a plant indigenous to the island, and its effects are both sure and fatal.

The Igorroté often carries in his right hand a quaint-looking weapon, which he uses for various purposes, one being to clear his way through any dense forest or jungle, another to portion out the spoils, and a third to act as a means of defence in a hand-to-hand encounter with the enemy.

The bracelets round his wrists, and the ornaments below the knee, are always of gold, when the wearer can afford it, and amongst the poorer classes, of beads, shells, or the twisted bark of some favourite tree. The use of these is considered indispensable, as they are regarded in the light of charms or talismans.

I believe the more savage of this extraordinary people wear no clothing whatever—neither man, woman, nor child; only the more civilized of the women wearing a kind of loose dress, sufficient to conceal a great portion of their persons. They carry their children slung on their shoulders by means of a handkerchief, or the knotted fibres of some large leaf.

The Igorroté is said to have no religion. They are married when children, but are only nominally man and wife until they arrive at maturity. The same Spanish author I have before referred to gives a description of a favourite dance, called by them "acubac." The men form a circle, putting their arms round each others' waists, and, placing all their wives and daughters in the centre, they begin to dance round and round them, shouting and stamping with their feet, to keep time to the music, which for this especial dance is called "inalug," and is a monotonous, dull continuation of sounds produced by their native instruments.

There are quantities of boa-constrictors in all parts of Luzon, and, in some instances, they are very destructive, though not, I believe, to the extent they have been described.

There are some stuffed specimens in the Museum, a small building in Manilla, containing some trophies from Cochin China and a collection of stuffed birds, which Colonel Créos has lent great aid in arranging and classifying.

Not far from here is situated the Academy, which is an excellent institution for instructing native artists; certainly meriting greater encouragement at the hands of the Spanish Government. Many of the oil paintings and crayon drawings were very well executed, and those representing the Chinese and Indian natives singularly correct and admirably finished, though defects might be occasionally detected, here and there, in the development of the muscles. When, however, we take into consideration that these youths have drawn their subjects from life, and that without any previous knowledge of anatomical drawing, these early attempts may be considered as astonishing, and very encouraging to the present Professor of the Academy, who complains of many difficulties he has to contend with in obtaining fit subjects from Spain for copies, the pupils requiring proper models for their instruction in anatomy—which branch of drawing, so essential for painters from life, the former professors, it appears, entirely neglected.

The Chinese have a great objection to serve as models, notwithstanding the good pay they receive for a task which is by no means an arduous one. This antipathy originates in a superstitious notion they have, that ere the picture is finished the sitter must fall ill or die.

One of these long-tailed gentlemen was on one occasion prevailed upon to attend, and sit as a model for a cake-vendor, his scruples being partially overcome by the promise of eight dollars. All went on very well until the artist, in great glee at his success, told his companions that the picture now only required a few finishing touches. Unfortunately, just at this juncture, the Chinaman happened, in the midst of conversation, to relate to a friend of his, a shopkeeper on the Escolta, his regular attendance at the Academy, and the favourable result of the sittings.

"What!" said the friend, "are you having your likeness taken? Do you not know that it is about the most unlucky thing you can possibly do?"

"Yes," replied the Chinese model, "I know

well it is said to be so, but I have found no bad effects, and therefore I begin to think it is all nonsense."

" Well, think as you like, my friend," said the tradesman, elevating his eyebrows, and endeavouring to open his small, elongated eyes a little wider, " but so sure as you continue your sittings, so surely will you be a dead man when the picture is completed; do you not now feel unwell? Your eyes look very heavy and feverish."

" Now you speak of it," answered the man, in a melancholy tone, and with a very woe-begone expression of countenance, "I have, I remember well, suffered more lately from headache, and last night I had a slight twinge of pain in my stomach. No doubt these are the forerunners of approaching disease and death. I'll go no more, and only hope I have not given up too late."

It may be well here to add that the Escolta is the part of the town especially abounding in Chinese shops. It is a fine open street, and the shops present a very gay appearance, with their active, indefatigable inmates, ever on the alert to make money. The greater part of the inhabitants of Manilla sleep for an hour or two in the middle of the day; but these industrious emigrants never seem to require any repose until late at night, when there exists no longer a chance of "turning a penny."

Each province has a governor, called in Spanish "El Gobernadorcillo," who acts in Luzon as an Alcalde does in the mother country. He has only a very limited income, but being allowed to trade, generally makes a nice thing of it. His dress is very singular, as he wears a European shirt outside his trowsers. All the mestizos do this, because the Spaniards are pleased with any peculiarity of dress that distinguishes them from the other inhabitants. The style of shirt, however, is not exactly European, but more like a jacket, and made of peña, often beautifully embroidered, so that it does not present such a very odd appearance, though worn outside.

The mestizo is decidedly, on the whole, a great improvement on the Tagalo, their features being generally so much better, and more resembling those of the Spaniards, while the long hair of the women, often falling in luxuriant wavy masses, instead of the straight lanky tresses of the native, and very often, too, of a finer quality, almost rivals that of the Spanish women themselves.

Robberies are very frequent throughout the

whole of the Philippines, but the culprits are rarely brought to justice. In fact, there exists a well-known band, or bands we may say, of brigands, called Tulisans; and though they venture close to Manilla, and are in many cases well known, they are rarely seized. Why, remains to be explained; but, unfortunately, I can only draw my own conclusions, as others do. The reason for such leniency is best known to the high authorities themselves. My opinion is that many an acknowledged Tulisan occupies the place of an honest man, and while seemingly against the brigands, is secretly in league with them, receiving, it may be, a reward for defeating the ends of justice. Many of the farmers, I know, are perfectly cognizant of their haunts, and owe their safety to overlooking acts of misdemeanour on the part of these powerful bands. One farmer told us, whilst we were travelling in the interior, that he let out some of his land to the Tulisans, and that they supplied him with contraband tobacco. On one occasion, when we wished to make an excursion, from which, as the thieves abounded about that part, some friends had attempted to turn us, another farmer assured us we were perfectly safe; "for," said he, "I will send a man with you, and I declare not a Tulisan would touch a hair of the head of me or mine." They generally prefer robbing the rich native or mestizo to attacking Europeans; but even these do not always escape. A lady in Manilla, I was told, was once driving some distance from town, in the dusk of evening, when her carriage was suddenly surrounded, and she was politely requested to dismount and accompany them; and some days after, when they had deprived her of all that was valuable belonging to her, she was brought back to her own house.

A very influential Chinese merchant was likewise stopped on his return from Maraquinha, his carriage and horses detained, his person thoroughly searched, and, after he had been robbed of all worth taking, he was suffered to return alone to Manilla on foot.

A band of those lawless ruffians once pillaged a vessel near the shore, and murdered the crew. The Gobernadorcillo for the province where the offence was committed, offered a reward of five hundred dollars for the apprehension of each of these murderers. A mestizo whom we knew, having formed the resolution to gain some of this money, set his wits to work in order to devise some scheme for obtaining what he wished. After some trouble he found a boy who knew the parties he was in search of. Having well bribed him, he bade him try to obtain the confidence of some of the gang, and to tempt them by the prospect of imaginary wealth to be gained by robbing his house. The deluded banditti fell into the snare, and entered the house at night, guided by their false friend. Immediately securing all the doors and windows, the mestizo, according to his own statement, armed only with a revolver, entered the room where they considered themselves concealed. At first they presented their carbines in order to terrify him, but on finding out the real state of affairs, that they had been betrayed, and were now unable to leave the house, they submitted quietly, feeling sure that the whole premises were surrounded by officers of the police or friends of their captor. They were all apprehended, and being tried soon after, were found guilty, and sentenced to be beheaded. The mestizo received the reward, and very high encomiums for his courage and presence of mind.

A curious people exist in the island of Mindanao. They are quite black, and exactly like the negroes in Africa. It is supposed that their ancestors, being shipwrecked on the island, fled up into the mountains, and there settling, intermarried with the aborigines. They are cannibals, and very ferocious. On returning from any victorious battle, they kill their prisoners, and taking out their brains, mix them with cocoa-nut wine of their own production, and drink the horrid mixture, shouting, dancing, and grinning horribly all the time.

Having arranged all for our excursion into the country, we started one morning soon after five, in two carriages, our friend Signor C. and another gentleman accompanying us. About seven we arrived at a place called Malapatnabatu, which signifies, in the Tagal language, light-coloured stone. Here we alighted, and entering a small canoe, seated ourselves on a neat framework of bamboo, which was spread across the bottom of the boat. Passing by the village of Patéros, so called from the immense number of ducks which are kept there, we stopped to purchase some of their eggs, which the natives, as in Java and the Malayan Straits, salt in a manner very agreeable to the palate of those who like hard-boiled eggs, but which for my own taste I could not appreciate. After a row of an hour and a half, we came alongside of a large cargo boat, called the cásco—most probably because its cumbrous-looking shape bears some resemblance to that of a cask. These boats, notwithstanding their awkward appearance, go at a pretty rapid rate when the wind is favourable. They have mostly two sails, both composed of a framework of bamboo and ropes, the bamboo being in rows like a ladder. The matting is then fastened to this by means of strong black cords running lengthwise, about the space of an inch between each, the effect at a distance, in the yellow matting, being very pretty.

The whole deck is sheltered by an awning, composed also of bamboo and matting, the edges attached to the sides of the boat, except at the stern, where a space of about three and a half feet is left open all round, with sliding screens below, so as to be drawn up or let down at pleasure. The quarter is raised above the main-deck. We found it the coolest part of the cásco, a delightful current of air being produced by the continuous pleasant breeze. What struck me as most awkward and unwieldy was the rudder. This is of an enormous size, and whenever the vessel stops, has to be detached and dragged on shore, otherwise the constant working backwards and forwards, caused by the action of the water, would soon destroy it. It takes four or five men inside the boat, and two or more in the water, to arrange it again in sailing order, and even then much delay is occasioned by their frequent attempts and failures in fixing it on the hooks. When all is ready a pulley is fastened to the pole or shaft, and another to the side of the vessel, and then, by means of a rope connecting the two, the huge piece of workmanship is brought into play.

We did not get clear of the river for about two hours, or more, as it winds a good deal in some parts. We passed numbers of fishing canoes, which, at a distance, looked exactly like immense dragon-flies, the canoe being narrow, and the net, fixed for drying, resembling two wings.

Just before entering the lake we came opposite the mountain of Boso Boso, to our right; whilst in front, we could perceive Susun-dalaga, or the Virgin's Breast. In the fields, bordering on the water, we saw a number of birds, called Garsas, or Rice Birds, having a beautifully white plumage, with a long neck and legs, and a delicately-formed body, looking very pretty amidst the paddy-fields and marshes.

The Laguna de Bayo is very large, extending about thirty miles into the interior, though we could get no one to give us an accurate idea of its size. The water is of a very bad colour, and contains numbers of alligators, some of enormous dimensions. I was rather disappointed with the scenery, for, with the exception of the mountains of Susun-dalaga and Makilign—or Bent —the land is very flat. One island we saw as we neared our destination, the Isle of Talun, is a verdant little spot.

We had to land in a small canoe, which, being wet, by no means contributed to our comfort. We then drove to the village of Biñan, close by, a place containing a population of three thousand, where we were most hospitably received by Signor P—— and his good wife, a worthy, kind-hearted couple, both being mestizos. Here we slept on mats placed on the beds, which we found very agreeable and cool; the temperature, to my great satisfaction, being decidedly cooler than that of Manilla.

The house, like the generality of those in Manilla, consisted of two stories; the entrance being through a large door, similar to the *porte-cochère* in France. Then mounting two flights of a broad staircase, we are in the "caida," or principal room in the house, for general purposes. The whole of the dwelling part is confined to this story, which is surrounded by a verandah about four feet wide. Large doors, leading from each apartment into it, are kept, unless it rains, constantly open all day. The whole exterior side of this verandah, for about two feet from the floor, is composed of wood-work, with sliding frame-works reaching to the roof. These windows are not filled with glass panes, but with mother-of-pearl shell, cut in small diamonds, which, in broad daylight, look like dirty glass, but at night, seen from the outside, when the frames are all closed, and the oil-lamps lit, have a very pretty effect.

The lower part of the house is devoted to offices, store-rooms, coach-house, &c. The room we slept in contained an innumerable quantity of images, of all shapes and in all attitudes, while a number of suitable pictures adorned the walls. One of these amused us very much. It was an engraving of the Virgin, with six small square pictures surrounding her, figurative of her *miraculous powers*. One was a man in a well, clinging to a sugar-cane, which was apparently fixed across the mouth of it, and underneath was written, in Spanish,

" Por haber invocado à nostra Signora de Guia, libertose de una caida otro albanil que dando suspendido de una cana para no caer en no profundo de un pose."

" A bricklayer, losing his balance, fell over the side of a well; he clung to a piece of stick across the mouth, which saved him from falling to the bottom, in consequence of his having invoked the Lady of Guia."

Below this was another picture, representing a crowd of people entering a church, and these words underneath:

" Un sacristan de la antigua yglesia de nostra Signora de Guia, selibro milagrosamente de una caida desde la torre que dando suspendido del cordel de una campana."

"A sexton of the old church of our Lady of Guia was *miraculously saved* in a terrible fall from the tower, when clinging to the bell-rope."

The third represented a man lying under a stone, from the killing weight of which two men were delivering him. A priest, accompanied by two men, was standing to the right. Underneath were these words:

"Fabricandose el antigua Templo de nostra Signora de Guia, en Hermita, cayo un gran sillar solra un Albanil sin cousarle dano, porque invocó a esta Signora."

"Whilst building the church of our Lady of Guia at Hermita, a large stone fell on one of the labourers, without his sustaining the slightest injury, because" (says the Spanish) "he invoked the aid of the Virgin."

It was whilst we were staying here that I tasted the flying fox, considered quite a dainty by the natives. It is prepared, in the first instance, by being steeped some hours in vinegar, and then cooked according to fancy. Were I starving I could eat it, but should decidedly decline doing so if other viands were to be procured. It tasted more like very coarse beef than anything else I could think of.

These flying foxes are so named from the resemblance their head, ears, and noses bear to those of the common fox; but in every other respect they are more like enormous bats, the body often measuring ten or eleven inches, and the wings, when distended, being not unfrequently five feet across. Their wings are very singular, being remarkably heavy, and composed of a substance not unlike leather, which is, I believe, quite impervious to rain, and thus serves as a sort of macintosh in which, in wet weather, they can completely envelope themselves. At the extremity of these wings are claws, like hooks, by which they swing themselves from the trees. A colony of these curious bats forms a very odd spectacle. Settling in a number of trees, near together, they look, from a distance, like bunches of fruit hanging from the branches.

Next morning we drove from Biñan to Calamba, passing the villages of Santa Rosa, Pueplo, and Cabujao, in each of which there is a church, one curè and "coajutor," or assistant. Santa Rosa owns a dirty-looking town-hall. The principal vegetation here is rice. Doubtless most English men and women have read descriptions of the growth and culture of this grain, but for the benefit of those who have not, I will just give a slight sketch of what I have seen.

The sawas, or fields of rice, are arranged generally in terraces, or gradations, divided from each other by mud walls. The seed is first sown thickly in one of these, after it has been ploughed by buffaloes in water. When this is grown to the height of a foot, it is taken up, and a number of labourers, generally women, plant it out in the other fields, drilling holes as they go on, one after the other, walking the whole time about two feet deep in water.

We passed a few fields of sugar-cane. The canes, we found on inquiry, are crushed in the old-fashioned method. After about an hour and three quarter's drive, we reached Calamba, where we partook of breakfast, consisting of rice, bread, and cold fowl, which we had brought with us. Being Friday, neither the guide nor any of the other mestizos, except Signor P., would partake of the meat. He, on being questioned about it by one of his friends, made reply, "Oh! este es necessidad;" and, turning to my husband, he added, "I keep an account with the priests, so I will pay for this and get indulgence." My husband asked another if he also kept a paper, and he replied, "Yes," with a smile.

About nine o'clock we walked to the beach. It was very hot, the ground beneath our feet being quite burning, and, entering one of the canoes, we were, in a few minutes, on board one of the large boats again, and soon under weigh for Los Baños, which is situated near the head of the lake, at which place we arrived in an hour. It is a small village, situated at the foot of a hill, from which the inhabitants declare they hear a rumbling noise every night; which has led them to fancy that some day it will break out into an eruption. At present there is no smoke visible, but close to the lake there are some sulphuric springs, the water of which is quite at boiling heat. There is an old hospital here, and a bath-house, now in a state of dilapidation, though occasionally made use of. Why it has fallen thus into disuse, we could not learn.

The lake from this point of view is very much prettier than when seen from the opposite side. The land is more undulating, and the trees and foliage more luxuriant and verdant. From here we sailed to the shore at the foot of the Makilign, a beautifully green mountain, covered with trees and vegetation. Here my husband, accompanied by the other gentlemen, went on shore to shoot.

In an hour or two my husband came to take me on shore, whilst the others remained a while longer to continue their sport. After a short but rapid ascent, we arrived in view of the lovely little lake, which lay some feet below where we were standing. It is called after the mountain Makilign, and is situated immediately at its base, and thus completely hid from view whilst you are on the Lake de Bayo.

The flowers which grow all about here in wild luxuriance are very pretty, and many sweet-scented. This lake is said to abound in alligators, which the natives call cayman. My husband saw a small one, but I was unable to obtain a glimpse of their ugly forms.

About sunset we all embarked again, and returned to Biñan with our spoils, the sportsmen having shot some snipes, pigeons, wild duck, and a few flying foxes.

Next day we rested till five p.m., when we started anew for Calamba, where I spent a wretched night. The owners of the hut we slept in were poor, but very civil and obliging, and I should have been most comfortable—for we have been so long accustomed to "rough it"—but for my unfortunate antipathy to cockroaches and their perfume. When we arrived the inmates had retired to rest, and after we had ascended the rude staircase, and entered the room or garret above, we found the floor strewed thick with sleepers, some of whom started up, rubbed their eyes, and stared at us. I hope the scrutiny proved satisfactory to them, though they could see us but dimly by the light of the oil-lamp.

The good-wife left her sleeping babe, and shewing us into a small inner apartment, begged us to make ourselves comfortable, and then busied herself in preparing our couches, which were quickly arranged by placing mats on the ground, and pillows for our head. Then giving us a small cup of chocolate, the general beverage, she retired. The room we were now in was very small, and the only furniture it contained consisted of two broken chairs and a rickety kind of substitute for a table. The walls, floor, and roof were all composed of planks of wood, none of which were joined properly, and many full of holes. All this, however, was a mere trifle to the sickening odour exhaled from the cockroaches. With a sigh for my poor olfactory senses, I began slowly to undress, though this I could do only partially, for the chinks in the walls made us quite visible to any one who chose to look through. Before lying down we could not resist the temptation of taking a peep into the adjoining apartment. The scene was truly an absurd one, and reminded me of a hospital, though wanting in the cleanliness and comfort of those excellent institutions. Our China boy lay just on the other side of the wall; next to him was a relative of Signor P., whom he had kindly sent with us to act as a guide, and to interpret for us when the natives could not understand Spanish; then came the master of the house, a "rough-looking customer;" and beyond him again a young girl, a visitor. Besides these were other friends and relations, I concluded, and several children. Mine hostess had not yet retired to rest again, but sat in a kind of swing or hammock used here in place of a cradle for infants, apparently in deep meditation.

I had slept about an hour or more, when I awoke, and perceiving a huge cockroach close to my head, rose with a start, unwilling to have any of these horrid insects walking over me. My husband, alarmed by my sudden start and accompanying ejaculation, began to think we were surprised by thieves, and that I had heard or seen something of them, but could not help laughing at my discomfiture when I explained the true state of the case. I now seated myself on one of the chairs, placing my feet on the other, though, as they by no means matched, one being considerably higher than the other, and both being excessively unsteady, broken, and dirty, you may well imagine mine was not a bed of roses. However, the "longest lane has a turning," and though my uncomfortable position became still less and less agreeable as the hours rolled on, I endured it in sleeplessness and hope, longing for the morning, and selfishly rejoicing in the discovery of every fresh chink the daylight stealing through made visible, utterly regardless as to the feelings of the owner of the house.

Very tired I was as I took my seat next morning in the carriage, and very wearisome I found the journey to Tanauan, though it lay through a pretty forest, and some beautifully verdant coffee plantations. About half-way we passed the village of St. Thomas. The road was very hilly, and, as we proceeded at a quick rate, and had no drag, we could not but think our position somewhat perilous. However, we arrived quite safe at Tanauan, and partook of breakfast at the house of a friend of Signor P.'s. After this meal my husband accompanied our host, a sturdy-looking Tagalo, to see a cock-fight, an amusement much loved by the natives all over the island, encouraging a latent love they have for gaming. Every Tagalo has one or more of these game-cocks, on which he bestows a great deal of time and labour in educating them for the fight; and it is related, so great is their love for these pets, or the pride they take in them—I can't say which—that, in case of a house being on fire, the master looks to the safety of his game-fowls before he sees to that of his wife or children. I did not care for the sight, so I lay down to rest awhile. The description of this cruel amusement I will give in the form of notes gathered from my husband's notebook.

"The cock-pit at Tanauan is situated near the gateway at the entrance to the village. We entered the grounds and walked to the small hut, built of wood, in the shape of a circus, having an arena for the games, round which was a low railing of bamboo, to separate the actors from the audience. The umpire, on this occasion, was the priest of the village, a Tagalo of about forty; and this, I am told, is frequently the case. The parishioners like their priest as president, and I suppose the priest likes the occupation. A heap of silver dollars were on a table close by him, and at each end two vice-presidents were seated, one of them very energetic in trying to induce the people to bet, by bawling out, at the top of his voice, the name of the favourite cock in the ring, while the other was busily occupied in drawing up his ledger.

"On a given signal, two cocks were brought out—one a small white one, and the other speckled. The bets being five to one in favour of the former, the president called out, 'Sacuti! (white) sacuti has the highest bets! Bet on! bet on for the speckled!'

"The game now commenced. Two men, each holding one of the 'combatants' in his hands, endeavoured to raise their rage by allowing them to peck each other's combs. This done, they held them by their tails, and, suffering them to approach quite close to each other, withdrew them again, so as to aggravate and irritate them as much as possible.

"But now the full force of the game has to come on. The president signifies it is time to leave off trifling, and begin in earnest. Accordingly, a steel spur is fastened to the right spur of the cock, which is purposely kept short. It is like a miniature sword, with two rings at one end, one standing in a vertical and the other in a horizontal position. The vertical ring is placed on the natural spur of the cock, and the horizontal over the fifth claw. The blade, which is very sharp, being sheathed in a leathern case, was withdrawn when both were ready, and the fowls rushed at each other with all their fury. The blades were too deadly to allow the combat to be prolonged very much. The white cock proved to be the best soldier of the two. Very adroitly did he manage to elude every stroke his adversary aimed at him, till, choosing his time in quite a sagacious manner, he seized a favourable opportunity, and wounded his antagonist in the breast, which made the speckled one, a large bird, stagger and shake convulsively; but quickly recovering, and maddened with pain, he flew at the white cock, and inflicted a slight wound in the right wing—a desperate blow, but one that cost him heavily. By no means disabled, the white cock now aimed his spur straight at the stomach of the speckled one, stabbed him, till he bled profusely, and, perfectly exhausted, fell down, and died after a few struggles, Loud and repeated cheers proclaimed the termination of the game; and when these had sudsided, the president formally declared the white cock conqueror of the field. I could not stay to see a repetition of this scene, but left the place disgusted at the cruel sight I had witnessed.

"As I passed through the grounds attached to the cock-pit, I saw, to my horror, that already, though life was not yet quite extinct, the poor speckled combatant, lately so furious and active, was actually being plucked to serve as a meal that day for his master and family."

After an early dinner we prepared to continue our journey; but, as usual, we lost some time in starting, owing to the indolence of the natives, who are naturally very inactive and lethargic, and being governed by a people not by any means energetic themselves, there is nothing to spur them on to a greater state of activity. At last, when all was arranged, and the horses put to, we were about to leave the house, in order to enter the carriage, when we were stopped again.

It appears a procession was issuing from the church, and we had to wait till it had passed. It consisted of numbers of men and women dressed for the occasion. One man played the clarionet, making numerous roulades and flourishes, but no decided air; another performed on the violoncello; and others sang from time to time. Behind these, on a stand carried by four men, was a wooden figure, meant to represent our blessed Saviour. It was in a kneeling posture, clothed in red velvet, with a band of silver round the waist, and three silver ornaments on the head. The latter were meant for a glory, no doubt, but, being fixed upright, they had exactly the appearance, from a distance, of feathers, as worn by the Ojibbeway Indians. The figure was made so as to appear sinking under the weight of a large wooden cross it carried on its back.

The windows of the house we were in were decorated with candles in honour of the procession, which, from their gay colours, our little child, mistaking them for playthings, eagerly grasped, and burned her poor little fingers.

Turning from this sad spectacle of idolatry, now fading away in the distance, we entered the carriage, and were soon once more *en route*.

CHAPTER III.

AN ACCIDENT—LONELY WALK TO LAGUNA DE TAAL—PERPLEXITIES—THE FRIEND IN NEED—SUGAR FACTORY—NIGHT'S LODGING—TAGALO PREDILECTION FOR SEMI-HATCHED EGGS—SAIL ON THE LAKE—ISLAND OF TAAL—DESCRIPTION OF VOLCANO—VILLAGE OF TALASSIG—RUINS OF CHURCH—RETURN TO SHORE—JOURNEY BACK IN A BUFFALO CART—SLEEP AT TANAUAN—ARRIVE AT BINAN—PROCEED NEXT DAY TO MANILLA—SIGNOR C.—— KINDLY REMOVED ALL OUR THINGS FROM THE HOTEL, AND WISHES US TO STAY TILL WE LEAVE—DELIGHTFUL FORTNIGHT—DEPARTURE FROM MANILLA.

CHAPTER III.

THE road was very bad—hilly and full of deep ruts and holes—but still we managed to get over the half of our journey quite safely, perhaps owing to the numerous cautions my husband gave the driver, to whom the road was quite new, being rarely traversed by any vehicles but carts.

At last we came to a very steep descent, and, though we repeated our cautions to be particular, as we had no drag, the coachman heedlessly dashed on at a furious pace, and succeeded in capsizing the carriage about half-way down. Fortunately our horses were too tired, by a long day's work over rough roads, to kick very much. One fell, and the other remained pretty quiet, considering how it was tried. We jumped out, and walked to the opposite bank; and thankful were we to escape unhurt, with the exception of a few bruises.

The coachman fell from the box when the carriage upset, and sustained some injury. Our China boy ran immediately into a wood close by, and was soon lost to sight; but whilst we were wondering at his sudden disappearance, he returned with his nose and ears stuffed with cotton he had been gathering from the tree, and which served to stop the blood that had flowed from his nose. He looked the picture of misery, and would have it he was very much hurt, though, except for being terrified, he was but little worse. The sun had already gone down, and, by the time the horses were disengaged from the harness, and the carriage placed in an upright position, it was quite dusk, and "the shades of night were falling fast."

It was now discovered that the carriage was too much shattered to take us farther; and as we were far from any habitation we were compelled to walk. The Tagalo who had accompanied us from Biñan as guide was obliged to stay behind to see the carriage conducted to a safe place; as to have left it would have been to present it to the Tulisans, and we should then have been obliged to pay for its loss to the owner. Fortunately our spirits were not easily cast down; and now, being in a scrape, there was nothing for it but to " put our shoulders courageously to the wheel," and surmount the obstacles before us. So on we trudged, without a guide or a single soul to act as interpreter with the natives; for the village we were directed to contained only one man who could speak or understand Spanish, and it was his house or hut we were to inquire for.

At first we went on briskly—my husband shouldering his fowling-piece, the boy carrying our child, and I getting on as well as I could; for I now felt a great pain in my ankle, which each step seemed to increase, till I became convinced that, in the overturning of the carriage, I had sprained it. To proceed was very painful, to stay impossible; so, after a short rest, we went on again—my husband apprehending the arrival of some of the Tulisans, and I in too great pain to think much even of this danger.

We had proceeded some distance when we fell in with three horsemen, who, seeing our forlorn condition, signified their wish to guide us to the village we named. We could not but consent, hoping they were farming men, as they appeared to us in the obscure light; at the same time determining to be on the alert, to detect any sign of deceit or treachery.

After a wearisome walk of an hour or two, we arrived at the margin of Lake Taal. So far, so good, thought we. But now a new difficulty awaited us, for it was almost dark, and we had no idea which way to turn, as the men either would not or could not understand our wish to be conducted to the house of a man called Gonzales. After some minutes' deliberation between ourselves, we resolved on entering one of the fishing-boats close by, whose outline we could just distinguish in the glimmering light of the moon, and endeavour to persuade the men to take us to a village on the opposite side, where we hoped to find either a priest or some one who could speak Spanish. Just as we were walking to the boat, we heard the welcome sounds of "Buénas noches;" and advancing in the direction the voice proceeded from, we were soon close to a man on horseback, who proved, on inquiry, to be the very man we were in search of.

He told us that, while he was returning home, he passed the scene of our late accident, and being recognized by our guide, was instructed by him to follow us as quickly as possible, knowing what a fix we should be in.

Gonzales now took us quite under his wing; and, thankful to hear again the accents of a language my husband knew pretty well, and which I could understand a little, we gave ourselves up with delight to his guidance.

He conducted us to his house, near the lake; on entering which I started with momentary affright, for, by the flickering light of a torch stuck in a hole near the cooking-place, I perceived a sort of raised platform, on which was a kind of inner apartment, from which, with its body half-way through an arched opening, purposely made, stood an immense figure of St. Peter—its eyes turned upwards, and the hands clasping a couple of gilt keys. Quickly recovering my presence of mind, I looked around, and though the light was too feeble to show the entire place, I could perceive we were in a large roughly-constructed hut, where vats of sugar and molasses exhaled a strong fermented and saccharine odour. The small room in which the figure was prominently fixed we found to be the sleeping room of Gonzales, which, being surrounded by a platform, and the lower part partitioned off for the fighting-cocks, goats, and other domestic animals, had all the appearance, when lit, of an exhibiting caravan.

Our host, El Capitano del Pueblo, as he was commonly called, was formerly in the native army. He was a rough specimen of generosity and good nature. He very kindly gave us up his room, to which we mounted by means of a ladder of bamboo, and in which he spread a mat for us on the floor. Then serving us with rice, and warming some chocolate we had brought with us, he pulled the door to, and we retired to rest; not, however, without making an inquisitive survey of the interior of this dormitory. It was all made of bamboo and matting, with a wooden window, which was hoisted or lowered by means of a rope. I placed my hat on the stand where the figure stood, under the garment, which had greatly the appearance of an old dressing-gown, and we regarded with some curiosity the stiff row of curls, which was nearly all we could see, from within, of the head-piece, and which stood out at the neck about two inches in bold relief, looking like a row of formidable pistols presented at us. The floor was formed of split bamboo, each slip an inch apart; and our child, discovering some paddy, proceeded to amuse herself by letting handfuls of it fall below, greatly to the delight of the inmates of the farm-yard, as we imagined by the low chuckling noise they made. Here, happily, I saw no cockroaches; and, despite the rudeness of our couch, we slept well, being aroused at four to see the volcano.

Our host gave us each a hard-boiled turkey's egg, which we found extremely palatable, as we were very hungry. They adopt a queer method here with their eggs, which are placed under a hen for two or three days before eating them, as they think it improves the flavour.

We entered our canoe as the streaks of dawn fast ushered in the daylight, and were rowed to the island on which the volcano is situated. There being no breeze, it took us about two hours to reach it. On disembarking, we began to ascend the mountain, walking for some time on level ground. It is a bare-looking place, like all volcanoes on close inspection.

The tall, lank grass, which grows on the slopes and sides, and is called "talahip," assumes a yellow colour when full grown. Patches are then burned here and there, and the young shoots springing up afford fresh pasture for the cattle, which are under the care of a native zagál —shepherd—who, with his wife and family, receive from the owner the wretched pittance of three dollars—thirteen and sixpence—a year.

The morning was very agreeable, and the air cool and pleasant, especially near the summit, which we reached in less than an hour, as I was obliged to walk slowly, on account of my ankle. The crater is a very large one, being about five miles in circumference at the interior base. This we only guessed at, as we could obtain no accurate idea, but they told us it took a man twelve hours to walk round the ridge, and this, allowing for the difficulties he must necessarily encounter, might make it about what I state. It is very deep, and, in parts, apparently quite dry. The largest portion is a lake, the steaming water of which is a most lovely green, and the land close by of a bright yellow. Near this is a large aperture, from which issue dense volumes of smoke; and again close at hand is another smaller lake, where the water is streaked rose-colour, orange, and green. It certainly is a most wondrous crater, and very beautiful in its diversified colours. I should have descended into the interior, as we did into a large one in Java, but my ankle was so painful that I feared the exertion. So we sat down and partook of our morning meal—rice, cold fowl, &c.,

using our fingers, as we were obliged to do at Gonzales.

The scenery around was very beautiful, the lake forming a charming circle, not too large for any part to be concealed, when any one is seated, as we were, on the highest point of the volcanic mountain, which is nearly in the middle of the lake, and surrounded by numbers of smaller islands, all very prettily covered with verdure On our return, my husband shot a couple of ducks on one of these. The first fell and then rose again, being slightly wounded. Another fell, and as the men were pulling the boat towards the spot where he lay struggling in the water, an all-watchful hawk, or rather small eagle, descended, pounced upon the bird, and bore him to some distance, when, finding his burthen rather heavier than he had calculated on, he let it fall; but still, unwilling to relinquish the dainty morsel, he perched upon the body, and set to work eating his meal, quite secure of his prize, for we were too far off to molest him.

But to return to our view. The mountains of Maculot and Sungal are the loftiest to be seen, but numbers of smaller ones and verdure-clad hills are to be seen on all sides, with here and there herds of cattle grazing on the rich fields, or village hamlets " embosomed in tufted trees."

We were told the whole of the lake was, some two hundred years ago, a plain, but that the frequent eruptions since that time have quite changed the face of nature.

I have carefully translated the remarks of a Spanish author on the subject in question, and now present them, interspersed with my own reflections. "The mountain of Macolot, which we see to the east of the lake, elevating its lofty head above the others near it, was formerly connected with the chain of the Sungay, running opposite in a north-westerly direction. The portion now called the Volcano de Taal must then have been conspicuous near the centre of this chain, with the land on each side rising in gentle undulations, and covered with luxuriant vegetation. On these hills and plains numerous tribes of negroes lived, called Bon-bon. From them is derived the name of the lake, Laguna de Bonbon de Taal, though more frequently known by the latter part of the appellation."

The first mention we have of the volcano is by Father Gaspa de St. Augustin, who, in the year 1760, speaks of it as being a " mountain covered with verdure," from which we may infer it was not then in a state of active eruption. In 1707 the peak Binitiang Malaqui, now only connected by a small isthmus to the volcanic island, broke out in eruption; but notwithstanding the presence of an active crater, it was for some time still dotted here and there with luxuriant shrubs, "lozanos arbustos." In 1715 there was another eruption. Lava was copiously ejected, and in its downward flow made deep lines on the sides of the mountain, which appear as if they had been grooved with regularity and precision. At present this crater seems quite extinct. The peak is very conical, and covered with tall grass and trees from the summit to the margin of the lake.

"In 1731 the mountain of Taal, still in the centre of *terra firma*, burst out in a tremendous eruption, affecting more or less the adjoining hills, mountains, and plains. The former literally seemed to tremble, and the latter became an odd spectacle. Sand and water was thrown up, forming strange pyramids (asombrosos obeliscos), and the result of this was that the mountain became an island (un islote).

"In 1749 the inhabitants of the surrounding villages heard several loud reports, which they attributed to the firing of some vessel while passing the harbour of Casasay (situated near the town of Taal, in the bay of Balayan), following, as they supposed, an ancient custom, in honour of an image which is worshipped there. But it was not long before they were undeceived, for the repeated noises continued at intervals without intermission. The air became thick and suffocating, and the earth began to quake and tremble. The eruption burst out from all sides of the mountain, as well as the crater, and ejected immense quantities of earth and ashes.

"The sun was quite obscured, so much so that the people who inhabited the surrounding villages were obliged to make use of lights for three days. The earth separated in many parts, especially between the Laguna de Bay and that of Taal, where deep chasms yawned, and numbers of houses were buried. This lasted for three entire days and nights, but the crater continued in an active state for above three weeks; and then the fire disappeared, and nothing could be seen but dense columns of smoke issuing from it, which, however, for long after, was occasionally mingled with flames, only perceptible on a dark, starless night."

The year 1754 was remarkable for another eruption, more terrible in its results than the one described above. The priest, Bencuchillo de Sala, thus writes about it:—

"It was so dark in the vicinity of the lake that you could not see your hand before you. Ashes covered the streets of Manilla, though distant more than twenty leagues! The water of the lake was quite discoloured with bubbling streams of sulphur and bitumen, ejected from the crater, and literally boiling the fish, bodies of which were thrown on the beach by the waves, so that the air became quite impregnated with the stench, which, in consequence of their decomposition, they exhaled. Subterranean noises, like claps of thunder, were heard throughout all the surrounding provinces, and it was so dark, even at Manilla, that they partook of their mid-day meal with lamps burning. Matters continued thus for eight days, until all the villages situated near the borders of the lake were entirely demolished, from the repeated showers of pebbles, and enormous blocks of stone, thrown from the bowels of the volcano. All the trees and vegetation in the neighbourhood were destroyed, besides animals and human beings. The large river, connecting the lake with the bay of Taal, on the south side, overflowed its banks, flooding the fields on each side, and destroying numbers of boats and vessels which were anchored in the lake and river. The odour of the materials thrown out of the volcano was awfully bad, and, as the eruption lasted for more than six months, the consequence was that a terrible pestilence, in the shape of putrid fever, spread terror and dismay throughout the whole province, fully half the inhabitants of which died from the effects of it. The ruins of Taal, Lipa, and other villages (or, more properly speaking, their churches, for these were the only buildings made of stone), are still to be seen; the native huts being too slightly made to stand long in ruins."

From here we rowed to Talassig, to see the ruins of a church which had been destroyed in the eruption; and then started for Bañadéro, where we arrived about three o'clock, and set to work ravenously on our simple fare of hard-boiled eggs, rice, and chocolate.

"Would you like an egg from under the fowl?" asked our host, in Spanish.

"Under the fowl!" echoed I, "what do you mean?"

"Oh!" replied the man, his broad dark face expanding into a smile, "I offered you what we Tagalos think a great treat, a half-hatched egg. I have some now under a hen, quite fit for eating.

When I take these away I put more under her, so that we have a capital succession."

"But surely," said my husband, amused as much as I at this strange taste, "this kind of game cannot last for ever—does it not tire the hen?"

"Ah, si, si, Señor; but then, after taking away her eggs three or four times, I leave others for her to hatch, and then commence with another fowl. There's nothing like arranging these matters, Señor; but now, may I give you one, they are excellent?"

Declining the proffered delicacy, but none the less appreciating the generous motives which dictated the offer, we ate fresh-laid eggs, which we found very acceptable, and then strolled out to look at the sugar-factory—a small one, carried on in the old-fashioned method. The canes are crushed between two cylinders of heavy, solid wood, which are revolved by the slow circumambulation of four buffaloes, the first couple having the whole weight of the work, as upon their necks rests the heavy beam connected to and setting the whole machinery in motion.

The buffalo, ever a patient, though a most lethargic animal, is guided and led by a cord drawn through his pierced nostril. The untractable ones are continually pulled by their noses, "to make them go," while those more inclined to obey the frequent and exclamatory *dah!* are suffered to carry the cord of torture coiled round their necks. From the machinery above described the juice runs into pipes, and from these into reservoirs, from which it is taken and boiled in the primitive style. It is then put into vats, and, when coolly settled into sugar, sold to the refining factories in Manilla.

As no carriage came for us from Tanauan, as we had ordered, we started back in a buffalo-cart, prepared for a "thorough good shaking." The lake looked very lovely when we left, for it was fast approaching evening, and the clear waters reflected the mountains on their placid surface. Some buffaloes were calmly enjoying their evening bath, immersed up to the neck in water, looking so gentle and lazy, that no one would suppose they required a hole pierced through their noses in order to make them obedient and docile.

On our return to Manilla, our kind friends, the C.'s, would insist on our making their house our temporary home. Accordingly we "settled" at the hotel, and took up our peaceful quarters with this most delightful and most agreeable family, where we stayed until we left Manilla.

Tidings having reached the Philippines, during our stay in Manilla, that the Queen of Spain was *dans un état intéressant*, a *Te Deum* was celebrated at the cathedral, especially for Her Majesty, and we went to look at the spectacle. The regiments of the line present were in blue uniform, the breast-flaps of their tunics being faced with stripes of yellow braid, while those of the officers were embroidered with gold. The hats of the former were of large straw, covered with white calico, as a protection against the intense heat of the sun; and the latter wore caps, of very pretty shape and form. The governor was there, a man of short stature, with a very bald head. The music, as far as the band was concerned, was very good, but more operatic than sacred. In the vocal parts the bass voices were deep and clear, but the little choristers sang more like so many squalling cats than boys, which may be accounted for, perhaps, by the fact that they break their voices in these warm climates at an earlier age than they do in Europe.

We often heard the brass band playing very lively airs, on their way to, as well as in the church;

for musicians attend every ceremony, and all Sundays and saints' days. One ceremony, which took place during our stay at Biñan, was very curious. It was the burial of an infant. The body was exposed, and the nose painted white, which had a singular effect, contrasting with the dark skin. The relations and friends looked rather joyous than sad, and on inquiry we were told that, as the child "was already an angel," they held its absence rather as a cause of joy than one of grief, and therefore celebrated the day, not by clothing themselves in sable gloom, but by rejoicing, feasting, drinking, and masticating no end of buyéras.*

There is another volcano in Luzon, of considerable renown, which, I regret to say, we did not see; but I will give my readers a descripition of it in the words of a Spanish author :—

"The volcano de Albay, known also by the name of Mayon, is situated about six leagues from Manilla, in the province of Albay, and is said to be four thousand feet high. The town formerly called Albay now goes by the name of Legaspi.

"The first eruption we hear of occurred on the

* Buyéras, i.e., the beetle nut, and a variety of ingredients wrapped in a beetle leaf.

20th July, 1767, when, we are told, rivers of lava ran like molten lead down the sides of the mountain, carrying death and desolation in their train. For a while it ceased, as though to gather fresh strength, when, on the 22nd of October in the same year, it burst forth anew, and such a deluge of water was thrown out as to form rivers between Ibot and Albay, and Macacay and Malinao, some thirty, and others eighty yards wide, rushing on impetuously, and emptying themselves into the sea. This eruption lasted a considerable time, and when over the crater remained pretty tranquil for the space of three and thirty years; but in 1800 it burst forth again, ejecting stones, sand, and ashes. In 1814 a most fearful eruption took place. At Manilla loud and repeated reports were heard, sometimes like a great cannonade, and then subsiding into a low rumbling noise, whilst the roof of every house was covered with ashes eighteen inches thick. All who owned land in the vicinity of the mountain were much concerned and anxious about their possessions; for they began to fear, from the length of time this eruption lasted, that it would terminate similar to the one at Taal, when the surrounding country became a lake, leaving the volcano an island in the centre. Fortunately no such thing happened, but the destruction it caused was awful. Five villages in the province of Camarines, and a great portion of the capital town of Albay, were entirely demolished. Twelve thousand lives were lost, numbers were wounded, many maimed for life. The country around, from being remarkable for beauty and richness of verdure, became like a barren wilderness, every space covered with stones, sand, and ashes, in many places the débris being as much as ten and twelve yards in depth. The mouth of the crater was much enlarged, and on the south side of the mountain a new chasm had opened, discovering an aperture the depth of which was frightful to look into. In addition to this, three fresh craters broke out around the principal one, emitting volumes of smoke and quantities of cinders, &c.

In the year 1845 another eruption took place, and again in 1853, both of a milder description than the one above described, but still more or less destructive to life and property.

In this province there is also a mineral spring called Tibe, the mouth of which is nine yards in diameter and the depth twelve feet. When it rains in torrents on the hills, the water in this spring rises often to fifteen and sixteen feet.

One day, looking at a picture by a native artist, I was struck by the enormous size of the cigar thrust into an old woman's mouth. I could not help regarding it as an absurd exaggeration! But it really is not. Though these lengthy weeds are no longer in use, having, like all the varying fashions of the day, vanished into smoke, they were, only a few years back, greatly in vogue. We were successful in obtaining one of these monster cigars from a friend, though they are so rare now that but for this act of kindness I should have found it difficult to get one even as a " curio."*

I observed one day, in the hands of an old man, a curious instrument called a beetle-pounder. The mortar is of bamboo, the pestle being made of a small rod of iron. With these the old natives pound the beetle nut and leaf, together with other ingredients, so as to render them more easy of mastication for their toothless gums.

Here, as in Java and the Straits, the natives seldom pass an hour without chewing these favourite articles; and it is quite a ludicrous sight to watch a group of them thus engaged, looking like so

* The native women all smoke, and so do most of the mestizos openly, and I think I am right in saying many Spanish dames enjoy *quietly* their cigar or cigarretta.

many ruminating animals occupied in digesting their food. Those who are accustomed to it would rather go without their meals than this "luxury." When sallying out on a day's journey, the Tagalo will dispense with food, but never go unfurnished with this *viaticum*.

In the Province of Tayabas, we were informed there is a beautiful waterfall, called the Cascada de Botocan, situated in a picturesque country, and falling from a height of four hundred and sixteen feet.

Before leaving the Philippines the following little incidents were related to me:—

A soldier, in Manilla, who was fond of playing practical jokes on his comrades and friends, procured a human skull, and, fixing a light in it, placed it cleverly on a rat, which he set at liberty near the place where a comrade was standing sentry. The latter was so terrified at the supposed apparition, that he fell down in a fit, from which he never recovered, but died—not the only victim, by many, to such inconsiderate amusements.

In the street near where we lived, a number of coiners took a house, some twenty years ago, and set about their dishonest occupation. In order to avert suspicion, they dressed up a man in white, and sent him about the neighbourhood, at that time but dimly lighted. The alarm produced by his appearance was such that, for some time, the inhabitants were quite scared from that part of the town. However, this was not allowed to last long. Suspicion being aroused amongst the more enlightened classes, the magistrates made secret inquiries into the matter, and despatched a body of soldiers to inspect the house, where the men were discovered, engaged in their illegal proceedings. They were all taken and hanged; since which time no ghost has been seen in that quarter.

On the 8th of April we left our hospitable host and hostess and their kind family, our hearts full of gratitude for their attention to us in a strange land. We started about seven in the evening, in the steamer *Escano*, a *ci-devant* Scotch cattle-ship, now one of Her Most Catholic Majesty's men-of-war —very fit, I doubt not, for its former use, but not at all for its present one.

I was suffering from a bad feverish cold, and my husband was ill from sea-sickness, so we remained in our cabin nearly the whole way; and, but for some sago we took for our child, we must have remained almost without eating, for the food was execrable, and the attendance very bad. My husband declares he felt perfectly well until he partook of a dish at breakfast, the first morning, called "cusido," which is very good when well made, but in this instance was nothing better than a mixture of dried-looking torn-up beef—whose succulence the cook seemed to have appropriated before dressing it for the table; cabbage, turnips, carrots, and garabánças—the latter a species of small potato, very farinaceous, and much liked by Spaniards and Portuguese. This we could have eaten, but for an unwelcome addition in the shape of rancid olive-oil, more adapted to grease the wheels of a locomotive than to assist our digestive organs.

The captains of these steamers never dine with the passengers—in fact, seldom deign to look at them except with a glance similar to that they bestow on the cargo. They probably, indeed, regard them as little better than so much goods stowed in at Manilla, to be discharged, "wind and weather permitting," on a certain day at Hong Kong. Whether our captain did so or not, I can't say, but I certainly think we were served with the remaining portion of his dishes warmed up.

When in the retirement of our own cabin, no one ever came to lend us assistance, or disturb the serenity of our retreat. When we did require attendance we had to call out "Muchacho!" and knock as hard as we could on the inner side of the cabin before any one answered; for our own boy disappeared directly the vessel moved, and we saw nothing of him again until the anchor was dropped in Hong-Kong harbour.

The steward, or "major-domo," as he was called, came to see us the day previous to our arrival, and in a kind tone asked if we should like some dinner, as it was just served. This uncommon display of affability and good-nature at the eleventh hour afforded us not a little amusement. We asked him to bring some roast fowl, thinking, whatever it had been cooked in, we could easily divest it of the outer coating of grease, by skinning each morsel very carefully. Back came the major-domo with a fowl on a dish in one hand, plates, knives, and forks in the other; looking quite a character, his hair so closely cropped as only just to escape the term shaven. The upper portion of his portly person was enveloped in a jersey, and the lower in pantaloons, more resembling flannel drawers than anything else. In this costume he waited at table, and served the passengers; and, I verily believe, the same articles served him also for night attire. Having seated himself on the bench opposite our berths, he commenced carving the fowl—an occupation at which, to our surprise, he seemed to be quite a novice. At last, tired of the unaccustomed labour, he deliberately made use of his ten digits, talking all the time as fast as possible, to divert our attention.

"This," said my husband to me in English, which the steward could not understand, "accounts for the torn-looking viands we noticed at breakfast the other day."

CHAPTER IV.

THE HAPPY VALLEY AT HONG KONG—GO TO MACAO—"BREAKERS AHEAD"—ORIGIN OF THE NAME OF MACAO—REASON FOR THE FALL OF THE PLACE—THE PAGODA—A WOMAN TRYING HER FORTUNE—MODE OF DOING SO—CAMOEN'S GARDEN—MONUMENT OF THE BARD—EPITOME OF HIS LIFE.

CHAPTER IV.

ON our return to Hong Kong we went to see the Happy Valley, a perfect oasis in this barren land. The race-course here is the favourite resort for equestrians, being the only level plain in the whole island. It is prettily situated at the foot of ranges of hills, with a fine open view of the harbour, and the high pointed land of China beyond. A carriage road runs all round, and the approach to it from the town is by two routes. Trees here seem to flourish astonishingly. In one part we passed under an avenue of Lychee, Mango, and others, so fragrant that the air, as we passed, seemed quite laden with the perfume.

Leaving Hong Kong about half-past two the next day, we were told we should most likely arrive at Macao about seven. But alas for human hopes! At first we went on pretty fairly, for, with the exception of a few showers, we had a very good passage till within half an hour of Macao. We soon passed through Kap-si-moon, vulgarly denominated "The Cut-throat Gate," though whether the name is derived from its extreme narrowness, or from the number of pirates who formerly infested these parts, I cannot say. It is very pretty about here, the slopes of the mountains being much more verdant than near Hong Kong.

Our course now lay past numerous uninhabited islands, all more or less rocky. We proceeded, threading our way in and out, as through the paths of a labyrinth, so complicated seemed the route, and at last entered a broader expanse of sea, leaving the island groups rapidly behind us. As these, however, faded away others appeared in front of us, and about half-past six we gained the pretty group called the "Nine Islands." We were now informed that Macao was very near, and that as it grew dusk we should see the lights; but before we had reached a point sufficiently near to do this, there was a cry of "breakers ahead!" and the engine was suddenly stopped, not however before our vessel had stuck fast, and by a series of successive bumps assured us that she was quite settled for the night in her new position. Our captain, however, not being of that opinion, used every exertion to back her out of the shoal. This proving futile, he dispatched a boat out to sea with an anchor, which the men were ordered to lower when a good distance off, for we were so close to the beach that a skilful jumper would have considered it no great feat to leap ashore. The sailors on board, assisted by many passengers, then pulled hard at the rope by which the anchor was connected with the ship; but this likewise proved unavailing, the only benefit that resulted being that the vessel was prevented from getting into a worse position on shore by the rising tide. Very soon it grew pitch dark, and thus we remained till about ten o'clock, when the tide had risen, and with some extra labour in pushing, pulling, and backing, we were enabled to float once more, and steamed away, greatly to the satisfaction of all, into the inner harbour of Macao, where, taking a boat, we were quickly rowed to the shore. But our troubles did not end here, for we could procure neither coolies nor chair, owing to the lateness of the hour; and had it not been for the assistance of a fellow-passenger, I know not what we should have done. He sent to his own house for a chair for me, and arranged with the boat-women to carry the baggage. So that at last, about midnight, we arrived at the hospitable mansion of Baron de C——, whose guests we were to be; and a most delightful time we spent there, the baron, baroness, and their son and daughter-in-law showing us every kindness in their power. Their house is charmingly situated close to the beach, in the Praya Grande, commanding a fine view of the harbour, the islands in the distance, with their mountain-tops clearly defined against the bright blue sky, giving beauty and variety to the scene.

The origin of the name of Macao is thus accounted for. When the Portuguese landed here, the first thing that struck them was a little boy running to his mother for protection from a dog, which barking furiously, he kept crying out, "Ma, kow!" "Mother, the dog!" Hence, as is supposed, the name of Macao is derived. I was told by another that it meant "water lily," numbers of these beautiful flowers being found in the marshes about the neighbourhood. The situation of the town, with its surrounding hills and mountains, as seen from the isthmus which connects it with the mainland of China, is also said very much to resemble the same flower; the Chinese adding that, like the water-lily, "it will fade, but never die," rather a poetic idea for John Chinaman, and in one point true.

Until the year 1840, Macao was a flourishing town. The English residents, seeing the necessity for free trade, petitioned the Portuguese authorities, requesting likewise leave to build on a certain portion of ground close to the town. These demands being blindly refused, our merchants gradually left, numbers establishing themselves at Hong Kong, a place then of no note, but which in a few years became a bustling, flourishing seaport. As it increased in wealth and importance, Macao gradually retrograded, and it is now a place where comparatively little commerce is carried on; for though they have recently made it a free port, it is now too late to recover what it has lost.

In the time of Lord Anson the Typa, near Macao, was deep enough to receive the *Centurion*, a sixty gun ship; but at the present time I believe no vessels of a large size can enter, owing to the great deposition of mud, which has made it shallower.

Macao is an extremely prettily situated peninsula, not so large as the island of Hong Kong, but less barren. The view of the town from the new harbour is very fine. The part facing the sea, with its numerous European-looking houses, is known as the Praya Grande, and forms quite a pretty crescent. To the right is the Fort of San Francisco, immediately below which winds a walk up the rocks, running all round one side of the town, commencing at the esplanade, where the military band plays twice a week—Sundays and Thursdays. The Pagoda is a very gay-looking building—the exterior embellished with paintings and small figures cast in clay, forming one large subject, in imitation of sculpture on stone. On entering the interior, the first thing which attracted our attention was an enormously stout figure to the left, close to the entrance, with tremendous staring eyes and puffed out cheeks; by the side of which stood an ill-proportioned white horse, the heads of both forming the most prominent part of their bodies. This is Matankuan, the god of grooms, worshipped by all who are connected with horse-dealing.

Passing a small altar in the centre, we caught sight of a woman's head behind a screen, in the act of bowing before "Hon-chung-Kwan," the god of wisdom, an immense figure in a sitting posture, with huge staring eyes—very un-Chinese like, by-the-bye—and a mass of tawdry gilding. As the woman had a servant with her, I suspect she was a little above the lower class, though her feet were *too natural* to admit of her laying claim to the title of lady. After remaining on her knees some time, and bowing her head till it must have ached, she took in her hand two small oval pieces of wood, which she threw three times, then burning some pastille and gilt paper, rose, went to a counter, where charms, I suppose, were sold, bought a miniature sword, and left the place.

I am told they always go through this ceremony before undertaking a journey. The object of throwing the oval pieces of wood is this. One side of each piece being flat, and the other slightly rounded, if the two pieces fall on the flat side it is considered unlucky, and, however important may be their intended journey, it is deferred. If one falls on the flat side, and the other on the round, it is considered a better omen; but if both fall on the latter, it is decidedly lucky.

Two figures stand on each side of the Hong-chung-Kwan, supposed to be his aids-de-camp. At a book-stall in this Pagoda, a kind of fortune-telling pamphlet may be purchased. Picking out a sentence at random, the conduct of him who consults it is supposed to be guided by the precept it conveys.

Before we left we perceived some smoking dishes laid before the keepers of the place. I suppose they set-to heartily—leaving the care of the door to the porter, called Moon-Koon, which signifies door-keeper or watchman, who was sitting exactly opposite the god of the grooms.

The place called Camoëns' Garden is situated close to the mud-harbour, on a little eminence. It is now in a terribly neglected state. The ground is strewed with leaves from the fine Banyan, and other trees, which grow in wild luxuriance and beauty—the walks and paths are all in disorder—and everything wears an air of waste and of ruin. In this garden are some naturally lovely spots, needing but little aid from man to make their beauty more apparent, and to render their aspect less desolate. Huge boulders of stone are every now and then seen, some of enormous dimensions, poised upon others considerably less; and the whole seemingly, in many places, kept together by the clinging roots of trees, which twine round about them, assuming every shape, device, and form. It was a subject of wonder to us how these enormous masses of rock, around which all was green, came to be so completely isolated. Some of these have staircases cut upon them, so that you may ascend and see the view; but few of the steps now remain perfect, and you often run the risk of slipping your foot, and injuring some portion of your body.

Camoëns' Grotto is, in my opinion, quite spoiled by the addition of modern masonry. It consists of a solid block of granite, resting upon two rocks, through which is a natural archway, which formed the reputed retreat of the poet, and where, it is said, he wrote his "Lusiad." On each extremity of the archway are sculptured, as usual, numerous names, and many verses in various languages, some to the honour of Camoëns, others to the abuse of the name written immediately above, &c., &c. The monument to Camoëns is just within the archway. It consists of a stone pillar, on which is placed the bust of the bard, carved in wood, and coloured to represent bronze. Six cantos from his poem are cut into three sides of the pillar, and on the exterior of the rock a French gentleman has inscribed an ode to his memory. An ornamental Chinese wall runs half-way round this place, leaving a broad walk. You mount to the kiosk, at the top of the grotto, by means of steps rudely hewn in the rock, and, by so doing, gain a beautiful view of the sea and mountains beyond.

I have carefully searched, but can find but little concerning Camoëns. The greater part of his life seems veiled in clouds and mystery. A French work which I have lately read gives some interesting particulars regarding his life and writings. As little is generally known regarding him, the following epitome of his biography may not come amiss, now we are on the ground he has so often trod.

Dom Luis de Camoëns, the epic poet of Portugal, was born in Lisbon, some say in the year 1517, while others assert it must have been in 1524. His family was good, and originally Spanish. Simon Vas de Camoëns, his father, lost his life, and nearly all his wealth, by shipwreck; but his mother, Anne de Macedo, managed, by dint of economy, to send her son to be educated at the University of Coimbra. On his return Camoëns unfortunately fell in love with Catherina d'Atayada, a lady-of-honour. From this youthful passion dates all the misfortunes which so clouded his after-life. He was banished to Santarem by royal command, though for what particular reason I cannot ascertain, unless, indeed, it was his *affaire d'amour*. After this we hear of him again, as a volunteer, in the expedition which John III. was fitting out against the Moors in Africa.

He returned to Lisbon, after going through many encounters, wherein he displayed great bravery, and he now looked, in vain, for the reward, as a soldier, which had been denied to him as a poet. At last, disappointed and sick at heart, from poverty and unkindness, he sailed for India in 1553, in search of a fortune. As the ship left the Tagus he expressed his resolution never to return, in the words of the sepulchral monument of Scipio Africanus, "*Ingrata patria, non possidebis ossa mea.*"

He went first to Goa, where, not finding any suitable employment, he became a volunteer in a Portuguese expedition, in aid of the King of Cochin against the King of Pimenta, in which his courage was admired and commended by his superiors. He next accompanied Manuel de Vasconcello to the Red Sea, to fight the Arabian Corsairs. It is also said that he wrote some poetic effusions in the Island of Ormuz, in the Persian Gulf, where he spent a whole winter.

Unfortunately for himself, he tried to expose, in a satire, some follies he fancied his countrymen were guilty of in India, in which he treated even the viceroy with ridicule. He was, for this, exiled to Macao in 1556, where he was thankful to obtain the situation of *provedor-mor dos defuntos*, which, being translated, signifies, "administrator of the effects of deceased persons." However uncongenial this employment might be to a poetic mind, he was, at all events, secure from want, and able to save; so that when, in 1561, he was allowed to leave Macao, he had a small competence. But misfortune, which had set its seal upon him, seemed reluctant to part with her victim; for, on a voyage to Goa, he was shipwrecked, and lost the whole of his small independence, with great difficulty saving his own life, and the poem which was afterwards to bring such fame to his name.

The accusations of his enemies threw him, next, into prison, on a charge of "malversation in his office at Macao;" and when he was cleared of this, he was detained for debt. Succeeding, finally, in regaining his liberty, he determined once more to try a soldier's life, and accordingly went to Sofala, on the coast of Caffraria, with Don Pedro Barreto. Finding, when he reached this part of the world, that there was a vessel on the eve of leaving for Lisbon, he determined to forsake the profession of arms and return to his native land, which he accomplished, after settling some difficulties between himself and Barreto. Thus, after an absence of well-nigh sixteen years, this unfortunate man arrived in Lisbon, his poem constituting his sole wealth. He dedicated the "Lusiad" to the King Dom Sebastian, who received the compliment with evident pleasure, and in return bestowed a miserably small pittance as a pension, with permission for him to remain at court—this gracious consent probably being accorded because the poet, having lost youth and good looks (one eye having been shot out in battle), was no longer considered "*dangerous.*"

When King Sebastian died, this pension was stopped, and the author of the grand epic poem was reduced to such abject poverty that his old black servant, a Javanese by birth, actually begged in the streets of Lisbon to support the master in whose service he had grown grey, and for whom he had a sincere and lasting attachment.

The close of this great man's life was as sad as his journey through it had been full of vicissitudes. At an obscure hospital in Lisbon, 1579, he breathed his last, almost, we may say, "unknelled, uncoffined, and unknown"—so utterly destitute and uncared for was he whom Lusitania now honours as her greatest epic poet.

Besides his epic poem, Camoëns wrote many odes, sonnets, elegies, &c., together with three comedies, which are comparatively little known.

CHAPTER V.

FORTS—RUINS OF THE JESUIT CHURCH AND COLLEGE—A CHINAMAN'S DISAPPOINTMENT—ANGLING NEAR THE GREEN ISLAND—MURDER OF GOVERNOR AMARALS—ARREST OF A YOUNG ENGLISH MISSIONARY—RETURN TO HONG KONG—VOYAGE TO SHANGHAI.

CHAPTER V.

THERE are seven forts altogether on the peninsula: Monte, Dona Maria, Guia, St. Francisco, St. Pedro, Bomparte, and Barra. The principal, situated on St. Paul's Mount, and called Fortaleza do Monte de St. Paolo, or more commonly the Monte, was built in 1622. From it may be obtained a fine view of Macao, the isthmus which connects it with the mainland, the nine islands in the distance, on one side, and the Island of Lapa on the other. This fort is situated at no great distance from the Grotto of Camoëns, the top of which can be distinctly discerned from it; and surrounded, as it is, by trees, it forms a pretty spot, with the house of Mr. Marquese, the proprietor, just in front, all sufficiently in the distance to hide defects.

Just below the Monte are the ruins of the Jesuit church and college, built in 1602, and accidentally burned in the year 1834. The façade, which is left almost entire, is much finer than that of any other church or public building in Macao. It is in the Grecian style of architecture, and consists of ten Ionic pillars, with a principal and two side entrances. Immediately above are ten columns of the Corinthian order, with niches between for Jesuit saints, and one in the centre for a figure of the Virgin Mary. Above these is one intended for St. Paul, after whom the church was named, though, from the words sculptured on the stone above the door, "*Mater Dei*," it must have been originally dedicated to the Virgin. These figures, badly sculptured, and all more or less injured by fire, now look hideous. The body of the church has been turned into a cemetery, which, being already filled, and no space left for further interment, is now locked up and deserted. There is said to be a subterranean passage running from the college to the Monte, and from thence to Guia. Under the steps leading to the building are vaults, in which, according to popular report, great treasures are concealed.

A Chinaman, on one occasion, urged, I suppose, by the love of filthy lucre, boldly determined to penetrate into their mysterious recesses, and, raising some stones, prepared to descend; but, finding, after repeated efforts, that, owing to a strong current of air, it was impossible to keep a candle lighted, he abandoned the attempt, and set about repairing the havoc he had made.

A wall, wide enough to walk upon, runs all the way from the Monte to L'Ermitage de Guia. There are two gates in it. The one between the forts of Monte and St. Francisco, is called Porta de St. Lazar—the Gate of Lazarus—and that beyond St. Francisco, the Porta de St. Antonio, both of which are closed and guarded at night, and opened during the day.

The Fort, or Ermitage of Guia, faces the old harbour. Formerly, on passing before it, each vessel fired a gun, in honour of its military character. The view from it also is very pretty, as it is, in fact, from everyone of the forts.

During our stay in Macao we sometimes went out on fishing excursions; and having anchored on one occasion off the Green Island—Isla Verde—where our angling did not prove successful, we went ashore, and walked round the little isle, which, being a sweet spot and nicely cultivated, is a favourite resort for pic-nic parties.

One afternoon we took a walk on the high-road

beyond the city gate, passing Fort Guia, and going in the direction of the isthmus. The cemetery is situated on the left-hand side, on the slope of a hill called Pedra Paçencia, and is surrounded by a wall with little minarets at equal distances. Near this, on each side of the road, are two granite pillars, having the appearance of discarded lamp-posts, which were placed there to mark the spot reached by a Dutch force, on their hostile march upon the town, in the year 1627. Fort Monte was at that time defended by the Jesuits, a shot from one of whose guns killing, or wounding, the Dutch admiral, his followers were seized with such a panic that they retreated, in great haste and disorder, to their ships lying at anchor in the bay.

The year 1849 was marked by two very tragical events. Amarals, then governor of Macao, who was a brave and distinguished officer, and had lost one arm in battle, wishing to improve the town of Macao, proposed making carriage-roads in different parts of the small peninsula.

In carrying out these beneficial improvements, the workmen were obliged to cut through some of the ancient burial-places of the Chinese, which so enraged these revengeful and cruel people, that they determined to waylay and murder the author of their grievance.

As he was one afternoon taking a ride in the direction of the isthmus, accompanied by his aid-de-camp, Lieutenant Leite—the gentlemen and servants forming his retinue being at some distance—he was surprised, on arriving at a part of the road skirted on one side with low bushes, by the sudden appearance of half-a-dozen, or more, hostile Chinamen. Unfortunately, before they could summon the rest of the party to their aid, one of the villains wrested the bridle from the hand of the helpless governor, whilst others dragged him from his horse, cut off his head and remaining hand, and then departed, leaving only the bleeding trunk to tell the sad tale to the other horsemen, who soon arrived at the spot.

The assassins were eagerly sought after, but in vain, for, notwithstanding the strictest investigations on the part of the Portuguese authorities, no one could ever obtain the faintest clue to the authors of the dastardly crime, or to the haunts where they concealed themselves from the officers of the law. It was suspected that the higher Chinese powers had some knowledge of the real perpetrators of the murder, as, after the lapse of some months, during which time the Portuguese had been unwearying in their demands for the severed head and hand of the unfortunate governor, these were sent secretly to Macao.

About two months previous to this sad affair, the tranquillity of Macao had been disturbed by a singular, and, in some sense, a foolish occurrence, which at the time caused an unnecessary commotion, and some bloodshed.

A young English gentleman, belonging to a missionary school at Hong Kong, having come to Macao to pass a few days, perceived at a distance, as he was walking down one of the streets, a religious procession slowly advancing towards the part where he happened to be. It was what Roman Catholics term the Host, which, being regarded with great veneration, is conducted with considerable show, surrounded, preceded, and followed by numerous priests in gaudy attire, with candle lighted and incense burning. On seeing what appeared to him a singular mixture of theatrical display and fanatical devotion, and which, indeed, seems to us a mockery of true religion, the gentleman, not making sufficient allowance for differences of opinion and religious belief, and for the sincerity, however mistaken, of those of another faith than his own, imprudently determined to show his scorn for a display which he regarded as utterly at variance with the simplicity of the true Christian faith. Placing himself, therefore, in the way of the procession, he obstinately refused to take his hat off when requested to do so. All unpleasantness might have been avoided had he but acted like many Protestants, who, not wishing to violate their consciences by any manifestation of respect for a ceremony of which they cannot approve, avoid every difficulty by turning into another street, from which, if so disposed, they can view the procession in peace, without being required to join in any of those manifestations of reverence and devotion with which the true Roman Catholic salutes the object of his veneration. But this gentleman, with singular want of judgment and good taste, not to speak of Christian charity, appears to have thought it his duty to make an offensive manifestation of his Protestantism, by standing, with his head covered, among the bowing multitude who reverently adored the Host. On being again mildly requested to take off his hat, or remove from the place, he expressed his determination, with a contemptuous smile, to remain where he was. In consequence of conduct so offensive he was very properly arrested, and locked up in the guard-house.

Captain K——, then commanding Her Majesty's

man-of-war *Dido*, which lay at anchor in the roads near Macao, on hearing that an Englishman was confined in the Portuguese prison, was very indignant, and immediately demanded that Governor Amarals, in the name of Her Majesty, should deliver him up unconditionally. The governor replied that, before doing so, he must consult the Ecclesiastical Council, but promised to give a final answer as soon as possible.

A few days after this, there happened to be a regatta between the men of H.M. vessel *Plymouth* and those of the *Dido*, at which Captain K—— was appointed one of the judges, Governor Amarals, and many other Portuguese officers, having also expressed their intention to be present on the occasion. On the appointed day Captain K——, after being present as a spectator, quietly left the place, and, taking with him a party of marines and some volunteers, rowed to shore, where he landed opposite the house of Mr. Patrick Steward, into which he entered, and, passing from it through an unoccupied house and garden, in order to avoid the principal streets, he arrived suddenly before the garrison, and rushing upon the guard, whom the sudden attack rendered powerless, finally succeeded in rescuing the imprudent Englishman.

In justice to both governments it must be mentioned that the satisfaction which, in consequence of the event, was demanded by the one, was obtained without reluctance from the other.

Returning to Victoria, we embarked the following day on board the *Pekin*, one of the Peninsular and Oriental steamers, and were soon off for Shanghae. Passing through the Lyeemoon passage—a very pretty and interesting sail, shewing more than one entire side of the Island of Hong Kong—we perceived fresh houses springing up in all directions. We had a very pleasant voyage, often catching glimpses of land, and obtaining views of many pretty rocks and islands. On the third day of our passage, those amongst us who loved the picturesque were particularly struck by the fine bold-looking appearance of the rock or Island of Taychow. On the morning of the fourth day we entered the Yangtsi River, the name of which, signifying " Child of the Ocean," struck us as a very poetical idea, considering that it came from these unimaginative-looking people, who, I find, have bestowed on other localities names equally sweet and poetic in their signification.

The river is very broad, but the water yellow and dirty-looking. As it grew narrower we could see the banks on either side, which are flat, but well cultivated. About half-past two P.M. we reached Woo-sung. Some miles before approaching this place, situated on the right bank, there was a battery, which looked like an embankment green with moss or grass. It runs right up to the Chinese town, and has embrasures, but only one or two guns were to be seen in them.

A few miles beyond, on the opposite side, we came in sight of an Imperialist camp, looking more like a collection of puppet-shows than anything warlike. The banners were waving, and the flag-staffs, which were formed of bamboo, bent to every breeze.

Soon after four we reached Shanghae, which, seen from the harbour, presents quite a novel aspect, after Hong Kong and Macao. It is quite flat, and the European houses look heavier and more substantial, and in some cases are very fine-looking buildings.

We were most kindly welcomed by Mr. and Mrs. R., with whom we stayed till we left for Japan.

CHAPTER VI.

DESCRIPTION OF SHANGHAE—THE EUROPEAN SETTLEMENTS—COOLIES CARRYING PARCELS—PIGEON ENGLISH—CHINESE ANECDOTES—BOATS—MANNER OF BURYING THE DEAD—THE TROOPS—ATTACK ON THE NORTH GATE—CHIN-CHILLING THE GROUND—MODE OF BUILDING—WALL OF THE CITY—FILTHY SIGHTS—WALK THROUGH SHANGHAE — RESTAURANTS — MARRIAGE CEREMONIES — JOSS HOUSES.

CHAPTER VI.

SHANGHAE is now divided into separate parts. The town itself is entirely surrounded by a high wall, in which there are three or four gates, and on the top of which one can walk and inspect the city below. This, indeed, is the most pleasant way of doing so, for the town being inhabited solely by Chinese, and the streets being excessively narrow and filthy, a walk in any of the thoroughfares is very offensive to the olfactory sense.

Europeans all live outside, separate portions of land being allotted to each nationality. In that of the French, which lies nearest the town, numbers of Chinese have located themselves. The English territory is situated between the French and the American, and is divided on either side by a creek and a river, over which are thrown bridges. The strand here is called the Bund. The coolies in Shanghae, as they carry their burthens slung at each end of the bamboo canes which rest in the usual way on their shoulders, make a peculiar noise, or rather a variety of different sounds, which we never heard in any other part of China we have visited. If two men are carrying a heavy load between them, the man in front will sing out, in a sort of falsetto voice, *he-ko*, to which the other will respond by *hi-ho*, or *ho-ke*, as the case may be, in a kind of broken bass; both at the same time proceeding at a rapid rate, with the perspiration, when the weather is at all warm, standing in little beads on their foreheads, or streaming down their face and body. In the busy time of the day, when numbers of these labourers are passing and repassing your house, the incessant noise of their unwearying voices becomes very annoying, and it is only time that habituates the European resident to a nuisance which I cannot divest myself of the idea must be very fatiguing to the performers themselves.

Everybody who has read accounts of Hong Kong and Shanghae must be acquainted with the meaning of the term, "pigeon English." It is that strange speech spoken by those who, in the belief that they are speaking our powerful and expressive language, systematically murder, not without a considerable amount of previous torture, the Queen's English. It is quite a puzzle to understand it. Many of the words bear no resemblance to those of any language I have ever heard, and it would puzzle the most profound linguist to trace them to their origin. A dictionary of this original Anglo-Chinese would be inestimable to the newly arrived English traveller or merchant. The first attempts at conversation in "pigeon English," or English talkee, are enough to take the conceit out of a man who supposes he has a fair knowledge of all the varieties of his mother tongue.

The Chinese experience considerable difficulty in the pronunciation of the letter R. On one occasion the boy of the house, in some part of China which we were visiting, appeared before me with the following message: "Mem, want catchee lice for Missy Losy dinner?" which, being interpreted, signifies, "Mem, want rice for Miss Rose's dinner?" As may be well imagined, I could scarcely suppress a smile as I replied in the affirmative.

Missy Losy or Lose was the only way they could pronounce our little girl's name.

A gentleman told us an amusing anecdote, which happened to a friend of his. In all cases where the porter does not understand English writing, it is the custom for the comprador (a sort of cashier, or steward, employed in every counting house) to put the address in Chinese next to its equivalent in English. A gentleman once sent a letter with such a duplicate address to a friend, and the individual for whom it was intended being able to read Chinese characters (a rare circumstance, owing to its great difficulty) was frightfully horrified when, on translating the address, he found that the words on the envelope were, "To the red-haired barbarian," namely, himself. In great indignation he summoned the cooly, desiring him never again to bring him a letter so addressed. Whereupon the son of Confucius replied, with genuine Chinese imperturbability, "Suppose no put dat, Chinaman no sabi."

All the boats here, without a single exception, have large staring eyes painted on each side of the bow, "No can see, no can sabi," being the reason given for this curious custom. In the Yangtsi River, unlike Hong Kong and Canton, very few females are employed in rowing, steering, or sculling, all these offices being filled by men or boys.

There is a capital road to Sikaway, which was made during the war in 1857, for the easy conveyance of the wounded to the hospital at that place—literally to carry the sick away. Readers, pray excuse this most innocent pun! I believe there was a little difficulty at first in inducing the Chinese to consent to the ground being touched, as their dead are strewn all about, and a strong party stoutly opposed every attempt of the allied forces to carry their point, nor did they yield until we promised to restore the place to its former state after the conclusion of the war. But now, though matters have been arranged, and peace with the Chinese Emperor long ago concluded, the Chinese themselves, seeing the advantage to all parties, desire no change ; and the Europeans settled there are too content in the possession of this one good road for walking, driving, or equestrian exercise, to relinquish it without a struggle, if they should be called upon to do so. It is fortunate, however, all parties are agreed in their wish to let things remain as they are.

The surrounding country is like one large public cemetery, the custom in this part of China being, not to bury the dead, but merely to place the coffin on the ground, some leaving it entirely exposed, while others, according to their ability or disposition, have it bound in straw or matting, or bricked over and concealed beneath a mound which they erect over it. As these remnants of mortality are scattered indiscriminately about, they present eyesores in all directions; for what can be more disagreeable than the sight of broken coffins by the roadside, or the skeleton exposed to view in the midst of fields of beautiful green paddy or waving grain? We also saw numbers of jars containing bones whitening in the sun, the skull generally grinning at the top, supported by the thigh-bones crossed.

The mounds, which are very numerous, are of every imaginable shape and size, raised in all kinds of places, without the least regard to order or regularity. We were told that during the time when the rebels approached quite close to Shanghae, these were first-rate places of concealment, from which the combatants could fire without risk to themselves; thus forming at once a resting place for the dead and a shelter for the living. Were it not for this unpleasant drawback, the country around, though too flat for the picturesque, looks rich in an agricultural point of view.

About half-way to Sikaway is a well which is never dry, a spring issuing perennially from the earth, called the Bubbling Well. Whether it is sulphureous or not I do not know, but I believe not.

During our stay in Shanghae the place was quite gay, in consequence of the constant arrival and departure of troops; and we often walked to the canal side, near the drawbridge dividing the American from the English settlement, to see the boats unloading their cargoes of loot and treasures gained in the various expeditions against the Taipings, the proceeds of which, after they have been regularly sold by auction, are fairly divided among the officers and soldiers.

On the night of the 1st of May, 1862, the North Gate of the city was attacked by a party of the rebels, and had it not been for the vigilance of our Punjaub or Sikh soldiers, then guarding that part of the wall, the men, who had been despatched from the rebel camp for the express purpose of burning the city, would, in all human probability, have easily effected their purpose. One man was caught on a tree, attempting, by means of it, to scale the wall. The others, on perceiving the discovery and capture of their more daring companion, or leader, fled, after firing a few shots, which were answered by the guard too warmly for their taste.

The man who was captured, a mandarin, was next day handed over to the Taoutai, or chief of the city, who questioned him pretty sharply. At first he maintained an obstinate silence, but at last was terrified into making a full confession; acknowledging that he was one of two hundred Taipings who had come all the way from Nankin on foot, for the express purpose of setting fire to the city of Shanghae. Although I cannot say I was disturbed by them myself, the shots were distinctly heard by many of the other Europeans, as well as by my husband, who remarked the circumstance to our host next morning.

The mandarin, who had so lightly risked his life for a bad cause, was beheaded the following day, within the city walls, in a field kept for that purpose, which, I was told, presented sometimes a frightful appearance, from the number of victims there slaughtered. It is remarkable how calmly these people await death, presenting their necks to the knife of the executioner, who cuts off head after head with astonishing dexterity and quickness.

A portion of the compound belonging to the house we resided in having been sold to a Chinaman for building purposes, he began very actively to uproot the trees, measure out the ground, and fill the space near the gate with bricks and mortar, not forgetting, however, previous to commencing operations, certain formal proceedings which are generally gone through, and which we watched with considerable interest and amusement.

As the labourers chalked out the line of demarcation, a tray, on which certain comestibles were arranged, was placed on the ground. A piece of boiled pork stood in the centre, and on one side a boiled chicken, the whole body of which was covered with a kind of saffron-coloured dye, with its head pressed under the two wings, which were brought forward, having a few long feathers left sticking out at each end, so as to present a most ludicrous appearance when they were united above the fowl's head, more especially as some were also suffered to remain unplucked from the tail. A coarse-looking fish occupied the dish on the other side of the pork, and a number of small cups were arranged in front, containing a yellowish-looking liquid, called Samshu, which, we were told, was made from rice, and is, I believe, very potent in its effects. Besides these there were other dishes, or, more properly, saucers, filled with different kinds of mixtures, and a basket, which was placed on one side, containing a number of pieces of paper, silver gilt, to represent the sycee. This is what they term "chin-chilling" the ground, and is an offering to their deity, by which, in their belief, they secure themselves from any accident or harm during the time they are employed in the erection of the house. After leaving the viands thus exposed for a few hours, they set to work and eat them.

We used to amuse ourselves sometimes by watching the progress of this building, which they seemed to pile up as a child raises a house of cards, and certainly it was not calculated to resist much inclement weather.

The city wall is from three to four miles in circumference. When we were there it was strongly fortified, each gate being securely guarded by night and day.

Entering by the Port Montauban, which was defended by French soldiers, and turning to the right, we soon gained the summit of the wall. A great portion of it was guarded by Sikhs, after whom came the tents of the Imperialists, a drowsy, inactive-looking set, dressed in blue jackets bound with crimson, and with Chinese pantaloons of the usual style. A large round white piece of cloth, placed immediately in front of the breast, which, I understand, forms an admirable point for an aim, and on which were painted some Chinese characters, revealing, most probably, the name or number of the regiment, &c., to which the soldier belonged, was almost the only mark that distinguished them from their more peaceful brethren.

The wall must formerly have been very broad, and many parts still remain pretty entire, but the masonry on the inner side, which supported the groundwork between, has crumbled away, or been removed, and the mound has, consequently, gradually sloped off from the outer wall, making it, in many places, from its irregularity and narrowness, wearisome to walk upon.

The interior of the city, which we entered on another occasion, presents a most lively scene, but is so disgustingly filthy, that I cannot possibly describe it, but must necessarily leave it to the imagination of my readers.

Following our guide, we threaded our way through the labyrinth of narrow streets, or rather alleys, walking in and out of the principal curiosity shops, and peeping into every place where we thought there might be something worth seeing.

An opium-smoking shop attracting our attention, we stepped in to "makee look see." A ghastly, emaciated-looking Chinaman passed us at the door, and narrowly escaped a fall, as he slipped off that tottering block of stone which, half-buried in mud and water, forms the step into the house. Placing a few cash on a kind of table or counter, the shopman transferred them to a cup amidst a heap of others, whilst the lethargic-looking customer roused his energies sufficiently to take up what he had paid for. This was a dark thick-looking substance, like treacle, which the dealer ladled out from a large wooden bowl, and, after weighing carefully in a pair of scales, placed on small pieces of paper with scrupulous exactness.

The smoker then took his place amongst a number of others, who, ranged down each side of the long room, reclining on mats, were placed on raised platforms, their heads resting on bamboo poles which run down the two walls. Before each was fixed a lamp, from which, after having rolled a small quantity of the deleterious matter between his thumb and first finger, and then inserted it into the tiny hole, little bigger than a pin's-head, he lighted his bamboo pipe (about a foot and a half long), near the end of which was a small round bowl, into which the opium was put, and pressed down with a small thin reed. When all was ready, he placed it at the light, and drew vigorously, never withdrawing it once from the lamp.

Now was the time, I saw, to watch the terribly

fascinating effects of this powerful drug. The small eye of the haggard, weary-looking man lighted up with sudden brilliancy, and the melancholy expression of his face disappearing, was succeeded by a look of contentment, and even of temporary bliss. The smoke, I should think, must enter his mouth in great quantities, though, as only a small thin vapour escapes occasionally from his nose, his mouth never being removed from the pipe, the natural conclusion is that by far the greater portion must be swallowed. On asking our guide how much each of these little papers of opium cost, he replied thirty cash—equal to about two cents and a half, or one penny farthing of our money.

The Chinese silk shop is a remarkable place for neatness and regularity. We have one near the end of this narrow street, the shelves of which, arranged, with the utmost regard to order, all round the shop, are filled with silks of various hues, though of the colours we can see but little, each piece being neatly folded in thin paper, which is carefully pasted, leaving only the ends exposed. Should you desire to become a purchaser of some of these rich and costly materials—which are, in fact, well worth the trouble of bringing home—at least a dozen or two of these nicely folded parcels have to be torn open, in order that, before selecting any article, you may be able to judge of its quality by comparison with that of others. The bargain being concluded, the whole must be wrapped up and gummed as before, a rather tedious process, I should fancy.

As but few ladies walk in this dirty part of the town, I was evidently regarded in the light of a "curio." Numbers followed our footsteps, and at each halt we made, crowds gathered round us, as though they had come purposely to see a "sight," and were determined not to be disappointed. I remember, particularly, a group of boys, who, after regarding me for some time attentively, smiled with evident satisfaction at the penetration of one of their number, who remarked to the others, in a tone loud enough for me to hear, "Mem—mem—one piecy cow," signifying that I was of the female gender, cow being the term used to designate everything that is feminine.

We passed numbers of eating-houses, more or less filled by hungry individuals, mostly men, all of whom were eating, apparently with great gusto, the cups being raised to their mouth with one hand, and the chop-sticks actively employed by the other to stow in the food, an operation which is performed with remarkable celerity. We noticed that table-linen was an article in the use of which great economy was observed, one napkin serving for all to wipe their mouths on at the conclusion of the repast.

Hearing musical sounds issuing from one of these establishments, on gaining the spot we observed about half-a-dozen musicians entertaining a number of their fellow-countrymen, who, dressed in their best satin bajus, conical-shaped hats, made of pith, and surmounted by a deep crimson tassel, were enjoying a super-excellent dinner, there being at least fifty different kinds of dishes before them, all more or less greasy and unctuous-looking. This, we were told, was a feast previous to a marriage; a ceremony regarding which we may at present communicate some of the information we acquired during our residence in this strange land. The bride is sold by her parents, or parent, and on the day appointed for the wedding, is sent to her future lord and master in a chair, the door of which has been carefully closed and locked, the key having been deposited in the keeping of a relative or friend, who, with an air of importance, denoting a proud consciousness of the great trust confided to his watchful guardianship, accompanies or walks behind the bride. On arriving at the door of the bridegroom's house, the bearer of the key steps forward, arrests the progress of the sedan by a wave of his hand, and enters the door of the house, opened for his reception. After a delay of some minutes, during which the friends and relatives, as well as the assembled crowd, wait with impatient looks, the door again opens, and the key-bearer, who has transferred his charge to the care of the expectant bridegroom, reappears. Without any hesitation, or unnecessary bashfulness, the gentleman at once opens the door of the chair and inspects his purchase. If her face—for its beauty in the Chinese conception of the term, and her feet for their diminutive size—suit him, he gives her his hand, and, with great efforts at gallantry, conducts her to the principal room of his house, where both burn incense, bow before idols, and worship the memory of their ancestors, the parents following their example. The bride then retires for a few minutes, and all partake of a grand feast. The chief ceremony, in which both bride and bridegroom drink from one cup of wine, signifying that their union is now irrevocable, is then performed.

Should the bride, however, prove distasteful to the bridegroom's fancy, he at once relocks the door, hands the key back to the man who brought it, and returns to his own house, merely forfeiting the sum he had paid, varying, according to circumstances, from six dollars to five or six thousand, which sum the parents retain as their lawful right. This, frequently repeated, would soon impoverish any but the richest merchants, and as they are never allowed to see their bride before they open the door of the chair in which she is sent, it is not strange that they should sometimes repent of their bargain.

The poor bride, on the other hand, has no such alternative. Kept in confinement until she is marriageable, she is then disposed of to the highest bidder, and dispatched from the paternal roof, where all her life of limited joy, from childhood's innocent gambles to the pleasures of more sedate years, has been passed, where the gentle mother who lovingly tended her infant years, and guided her childish steps, is left to live out her lonely existence, uncaring and uncared for by the voluptuous father, who has, probably, long since discarded her for a younger and "fairer favourite."

The young girl arrives in front of her purchaser's house, and, with breathless anxiety and gloomy forebodings, hears the key placed in the lock, and the door turn on its hinges. If, after inspection, his purchase is deemed satisfactory, she becomes the property of a new master, to all of whose wishes and commands she must be subservient, her own feelings or inclinations being totally disregarded.

So abject is the condition to which the marriage tie condemns a woman in China, that she may be divorced, not only for any levity of manner, or impropriety of behaviour, but even for being too sickly or more than usually talkative. The ceremony, however, must doubtless vary in an empire of such extent as that of China, every different part of the country having its own peculiar form.

A lady in Macao described to us the form in common use there, one totally different from that already referred to. I will give it, as nearly as I can remember, in her own words.

Previous to entering the bridal palanquin—for there is one expressly used on these occasions, more or less decorated and gilt, according to the wealth and station of the parties—the bride is made to walk over a small caldron of burning charcoal. At the same time, her mother presents her with a handful of rice, her last meal under the paternal roof. The farewells are said, the partings are over, and the young girl enters her chair. On reaching the house of the intended bridegroom, the bride is shown to a room, where are deposited the boxes containing her trousseau, &c., upon one of which she sits to receive her "futuro," closely veiled, and, doubtless, trembling in every limb. Entering, after a few moments' delay, fan in hand, eager to behold his purchase, he raises the veil which conceals her features, gazes for some seconds on the bashful maiden, and, if satisfied with her appearance, places the fan at the back of his neck. The matter being thus settled, the ceremonies proceed. If, on the contrary, he disapproves of her, he places the fan in the gaiter below his knee, and the mortified damsel is taken back to her home.

The next ceremony, in case the bride suits, takes place the following day. All the relatives of the bridegroom having been invited, tea is made, and the newly-married couple serve their guests; the bride being, of course, the cynosure of all eyes, and open to every kind of criticism. They then go to the joss-house, and all make "chin-chin-joss." When night comes on small candles are stuck about the wooden floor, which, being lighted, the young bride is made to pick her steps between them, a task of great difficulty, during the performance of which the guests examine narrowly her poor deformed feet. The last probationary duty imposed on her is that of cutting out flowers, &c., in paper. If she shows herself sufficiently expert in this ornamental accomplishment to satisfy the taste of those who are watching her performance with critical eyes, the general approbation with which she meets probably makes up in some measure for the severity of the ordeal through which she has had to pass.

Farther on we arrived opposite the largest joss-house, and, passing through a sort of chamber, found ourselves in an open court; traversing which, we entered a door near the end, where we saw a kind of altar, with a small figure dressed in blue upon it. This figure, which was encircled with a girdle, made, apparently, to represent precious stones, reminded me of the pictures of some of the Jewish high-priests. Behind it, besides other figures, were three gilt images in cases, of which we could see only the heads through little glass windows, let in just before the faces. The priests, or bonzes, with their shaven heads, and plain grey garments, stood about, apparently having but little to occupy their time. I am told these individuals are, in general, very little respected by the people.

Passing on through a door to the left, we ascended a flight of steps, and entered a lofty temple, down each side of which were ranged against the wall, some feet above the ground, nine gilt figures in sitting postures. Opposite the windows were seven gigantic figures on a raised platform, the ground of which was made to represent clouds. The one in the centre, which was painted, not gilt, and had a crown on the head, and garments of a most costly description, was seated. The two figures nearest each end were adorned with a kind of patchwork, formed of pieces of Chinese embroidery. Before them was an immense screen, or wall, running up to the roof, on the other side of which was seated their principal image, called Shilevah, of enormous proportions, all gilt, with a figure in an attitude of devotion on each side. In front of all were stands for tapers, which are burned as in Roman Catholic churches, two large, elaborately painted ones being fixed in candlesticks on each side. The usual immense bell and gong were fixed up to the right and left before the altar.

Our guide now led us back again through the smaller temple, and by another door, into a chamber in which were other figures. From thence, entering a species of corridor, we saw before us the "bad images," or representations of evil spirits, ranged on raised platforms against the wall; a figure of the devil standing at the end, almost covered with gilt papers, made to represent silver sycee, which the natives offer to him. On the raised platform, opposite the windows, were arranged about a dozen, or more, gilt figures, with wicked-looking faces; and below them numbers of small figures, representing, I suppose, imps of different kinds and forms, some with the heads of animals, and others red, green, or black, with white horns. The scene probably represented a species of Chinese purgatory, as numbers of these monsters were evidently torturing different victims. One figure, like a human being, was represented as undergoing the awful process of being sawn in two, while another appeared to have been deprived of his limbs, a third was suffering unheard-of torments in a caldron of boiling oil, and a fourth was seen struggling with serpents. Such, if he does not propitiate the evil spirits, are the future torments which the orthodox Chinese believer dreads, and, in the hope of escaping them, he comes here to pray, to burn tapers, and to make offerings to his deities.

One or two figures we saw almost covered with

bits of red cloth, and on asking our guide the reason, he replied,

"Oh! Chinaman come here, makee chin-chin-joss, for, if no makee, no good Chinaman."

It is one of the convenient articles of a Chinaman's belief that the good deities are sure to take care of him, but that the evil ones require propitiating, and must therefore be invoked. This is something like holding a candle to the devil.

No particular day in the week is set apart for worship, but different feasts are celebrated on certain occasions throughout the year. On the other side was a similar corridor, devoted also to the evil ones.

Besides these temples, near the street is a building containing three very large figures, which, as our guide informed us, being intended only for the worship of the mandarins, are not shown to strangers.

CHAPTER VII.

CHINESE WOMEN —MEN—LONG TAILS—PUNISHMENT OF THE CANGUE—SUPERSTITION—FLAVOUR OF TEA—GROWTH OF THE PLANT—REMARKS ON GREEN TEA—POPULATION OF CHINA, AND FOOD OF THE POORER CLASSES—BIRD'S-NEST SOUP—GELATINOUS FOOD—THE FORM OF SALUTATION—CEREMONY OF KOW-TOW—CHINESE IDEA OF GEOGRAPHY—THE EMPEROR'S HINT—THE TAE-PINGS, OR REBELS—TAKING OF KAHDING — CRUELTY OF THE REBELS — PALANQUINS—SAD ACCIDENT TO A YOUNG OFFICER—CHINESE CONVEYANCE—" BABY TOWERS" — INFANTICIDE—BIRTH OF A DAUGHTER NO CAUSE OF REJOICING.

CHAPTER VII.

THE Chinese women here, I notice, are much better-looking, in general, than those of Hong Kong or Macao; their complexions, in particular, being much better. Though I was told that this superiority is, in a great measure, attributable to art, as, indeed, I could easily discover in those of the higher classes I saw passing in chairs, or occasionally walking, yet amongst the labouring classes I could trace very often, through their filth, a more ruddy hue and a clearer skin than their southern sisters possessed, the faces being pleasanter in expression, the nose frequently less flat and the mouth better shaped.

The dress of the ladies is very modest, but generally gaudy. An embroidered light-blue silk dress, like a tunic, or large loose jacket, is fastened at the neck, and descends below the knees. Below this are trousers, sometimes of one colour and sometimes of another, but generally worked in patterns with gold or silver thread, the usual tiny ornamental shoe peeping out beneath. The hair is arranged differently from what I saw at Hong Kong, the form in which it is dressed not being quite so extensive. It is gummed and arranged at the back over a sort of framework resembling the handle of a tea-pot; a head-dress being placed across the front, very much like that worn by the Egyptian women, coming to a peak over the forehead, and frequently ornamented with precious stones, differing in value according to the wealth of the wearer. Flowers are also often worn, and silver pins are invariably stuck about, without any idea of regularity, but simply according to the taste of the wearer or her waiting-maid.

The men shave the front part of their head, and wear the hair at the back long and plaited. The Chinese, in olden times, wore their hair like the Koreans, tied in a knot at the top of the head, but the Tartars introduced the habit of wearing the tail. A celebrated writer ascribes this strange custom to two reasons—first, a wish to imitate the tail of a favourite horse, and secondly, the desire of distinguishing their own adherents from the loyal subjects of the Ming family. Many men at first obstinately refused to adopt this new and ridiculous custom, but each refractory subject was so terribly punished, that the rest, taking warning, submitted, and, singular to say, they are now so proud of this appendage, that the longer it grows the more it is valued, and one of their greatest punishments is to be deprived of it, thieves and other great criminals probably considering the deprivation of their tails to be the severest part of their punishment.

Although the punishment of the cangue has been already described by many previous writers, any account of this remarkable part of the world would necessarily be incomplete without some notice of it. It is composed of four pieces of wood, joined together so as to form a square, in the centre of which a hole, large enough to admit the neck, is cut. This piece of machinery is so contrived that it rests upon the shoulders; and the wretched criminal is thus exposed to public shame for different periods of time, according to the nature of his crime, the offence of which he has been guilty being written in legible characters on the board.

I am told it is extremely difficult to sleep or rest

M

with this torturing instrument around the neck, its weight averaging, in general, from forty to eighty pounds. In some cases the miserable sufferer has been known to fall down and expire in the streets from sheer exhaustion.

The Chinese are famous for their fireworks, which are really excellent. Those most commonly used are the crackers, which are frequently suspended over a railing for display, and go off in a string, one after the other, each making a loud report. According to Gutzlaff's account, gunpowder was in use in China before it was discovered or introduced at all into Europe.

Like all Eastern nations, the Chinese are excessively superstitious, placing much reliance in amulets, talismans, &c., &c., of which there are no end. A very singular one is made of old cash, in the shape of a small sword, decorated with a cord and tassel. This they consider one of their principal charms against the attempts of evil spirits to gain possession of them.

We quite expected to taste most superior flavoured tea during our residence in China, but were disappointed, probably on account of not sufficiently valuing the fresher flavour, our taste being so perverted that we preferred what we had partaken of at home.

Though they must appear like the repetition of an oft-told tale, a few remarks upon this inestimable shrub may, perhaps, not come amiss. It grows from about four to five feet high, and looks very much like a small myrtle, the leaves being dark and glossy. It is grown from seed, which is left in a kind of nursery for a year, or sometimes more, when it is transplanted to the general field, and set in rows, from six to seven feet apart, the leaves being ready for gathering the following year. It bears a little white flower, which some have likened to our wild-rose, and which is succeeded by a kind of small nut.

There are immense varieties of the tree, that of the green tea differing a little from the ordinary black, in the leaf, but the great difference in the flavour, we were told, is mostly attributable to the alteration in preparing it. Every other kind is put out in the sun to dry, whereas that intended for green tea is not similarly exposed, but at once undergoes the firing process. There is much truth in the general belief that *green tea is coloured*, as we have ourselves known instances of its undergoing this operation.

The population of China has been said to be very numerous, a statement which one can well imagine, from observation, to be correct, for it is evident that two Chinamen can exist in comfort where a single European would almost starve. They are so little scrupulous about their food, that literally it might be said, "All is fish which comes to their net." Rats, mice, dogs, cats, donkeys, and every species of vegetable, are alike partaken of and relished by them. Fish, dried, and kept till the stench is perfectly awful, forms a delicacy to eat with their rice. But it must not be imagined that this statement applies to the richer classes, who often fare sumptuously, and are, in many cases, quite gourmands in their way.

Besides the fact that Chinamen, generally, can subsist on a much less ample and generous diet than is necessary for Europeans, there are other reasons why one does not wonder at the immense number of their population. There is not, so far as we are enabled to judge, from the limited portion of the country we have travelled through, or of which we have obtained information, one square inch of ground wasted. The streets of their cities are narrow, and their court-yards, when they possess any, small and confined. They have, comparatively, very few pleasure-grounds. Every inch of land is turned to some useful purpose, their gardens even being intended not for ornament, but for profit or subsistence. Their fields of grain, &c., are manured in a remarkably careful, but cheap and disgusting manner.

It is considered quite a disgrace to die unmarried, and each man, besides marrying early, is allowed any number of concubines he can afford to keep.

We often partook of the far-famed birds'-nest soup, which, without the additional flavouring furnished by the cook, would be perfectly tasteless. The Chinese liking for it arises, probably, from their general *penchant* for all gelatinous substances. Many European residents likewise consider it both nutritious and wholesome. The nests are very expensive, being brought from the Sunda Islands, and taking much time and trouble in collecting. So far as we could ascertain, no one has yet been able to find out what their composition is; but it is generally supposed that the swallows pick up a kind of glutinous vegetable, with which they form their nest.

Another great delicacy among the Chinese is the bicho-de-mar, or sea-slug, of which there exist many varieties. Shark-fins, fish-maws, &c., &c., are all alike highly prized, and, consequently, from the great demand for them, more or less expensive.

Nothing can be more amusing than the observation of the various modes of salutation, and the ceremonies with which strangers are received in different countries.

The Chinaman meeting with a friend never shakes hands with him, but joins his own together and shakes them, at the same time uttering the Chinese " How d'ye do ? "

One of their most curious ceremonies is that called the kow-tow, which is only performed before the Emperor, who exacts it, not only from ambassadors, but from all tributary princes. On being admitted to the presence of the Emperor, they first advance and then kneel, holding both hands forward. Striking their heads three times on the ground, they rise, and repeat the same operation twice more. The music then beats time to a species of herald, who proclaims aloud,

" Behold what an act of submission to our Emperor! Witness the obedience shewn! "

This ceremony is also expected in return for any message, however unimportant, or any present, however small, which the Celestial Emperor may send. It is related that, in the year 1795, the Dutch embassy went through this humiliating ceremony, to testify their gratitude for the regal gift of some bones the flesh of which had been half-gnawed off.

The Chinese knowledge of geography must be very limited, for we were told that, even to the present day, they consider the earth one vast plain —China, of course, being situated exactly in the centre.

When the Emperor wishes to get rid of a troublesome courtier or minister, he sends him a piece of silver cord; and unless the obnoxious individual takes the hint, and commits suicide, his life is disposed of for him; the emblem sent being considered quite a sufficient warning, the object of which is perfectly intelligible.

The Tae-pings, or rebels, are principally composed of the idle and the lazy, in fact, the very dregs of the people; and no sooner does the industrious peasant cultivate his land and prepare to reap the fruits of his labour, than his rapacious brethren come down upon him, despoil him of everything, and murder, or make slaves of men, women, and children—horrors which the Imperialists seem to have no power to arrest.

The Tae-pings advance with rapid stride, dealing death and destruction around, and speedily reducing whole provinces to a state of anarchy and confusion. As, under such circumstances, we could not look on and remain inactive, the allied armies have taken up arms in the cause, and have already taught these rebels some salutary lessons, with great loss to them and comparatively little to the Europeans.

Soon after our arrival at Shanghae the troops returned from taking a town called Kahding, which they stormed on the 1st of May. The following description of the affair was communicated to us :—

Having cleared away, over night, the obstruction of trees which the Chinese had thrown across the creek, the guns opened fire about five a.m., and they soon perceived that their work would be light, for, in a very short time, the rebels seemed to abandon the south gate entirely, and a shell bursting over a house in the town set fire to it and terrified the inhabitants. Orders were then given for the boats to advance, which they did, till they arrived at the ditch which surrounded the wall, where, forming a bridge across, in ten minutes the ladders were conveyed over.

It was then perceived that Corporal Collins, of the Royal Engineers, had already gained the top of the wall, having scrambled up with no assistance but the holes the shells had made. He was rapidly followed by others, and ladders were soon planted thickly against the wall, on which two Chang-maous were killed, and about twenty shot in the streets below. The South Gate was then opened, and the troops marched in to the music of the French band.

Kahding was thus taken in an hour and a half after the action began. The English fixed upon a Pagoda, which is situated near the centre of the city, as a good depôt for loot, and it was left in charge of a guard of the Twenty-Second Regiment, indiscriminate plundering being strictly prohibited.

After waiting half an hour, in order to give the soldiers time to secure and deposit the valuables, the troops were ordered to leave, and, as they passed out, a guard was stationed to examine each man, and oblige him to surrender any article he might have taken possession of, as all was to be sold and the money equally divided. In one house was found a quantity of porter and cherry-brandy, and in another an English musket, some pistols, and a number of cases containing English and French ammunition.

Nearly three hundred ponies and a number of boats were captured. The loot was estimated at considerably above a hundred thousand dollars. Fifteen hundred prisoners were taken, fifty of whom, being well-known as ringleaders, were immediately delivered up to the Taoutai for punishment. Among the captives were one hundred and fifty women, many of whom had been branded on the cheeks with the Tae-ping characters. The latter were, of course, at once released, but several implored to be allowed to accompany their deliverers to Shanghae, their fear of again falling into the hands of the rebels was so great.

One soldier told us he had seen a poor young girl whom the Tae-pings, in cruel sport, had burnt up to the knees, till she was quite unable to walk. The rebel loss was estimated at from one thousand to two thousand, whilst ours was trifling. The poor inhabitants seemed delighted to throw off the oppressive yoke of the Tae-pings, and resumed their labours with cheerfulness and pleasure.

The same kind of chairs are used here as in Hong Kong, some ladies making use of open ones in preference, when it is not too warm or wet.

The coolies are, generally, very sure-footed, but should the front one slip, you run a chance of an ugly fall.

A young officer, Lieutenant Wilson, was killed in the following manner. He was smoking his cigar in one of the palanquins, and leaning forward so as to rest his arms on the front part of the conveyance, when the front cooly lost his footing, and the unfortunate young man fell out, knocking his head against a stone. The two bearers, perceiving him lying prostrate, became frightened, and ran away. The officer was thus left uncared for in the streets of Shanghae, till, fortunately, a military doctor, who happened to be passing by, saw him, and had the senseless body conveyed to the nearest place of shelter, where he was carefully tended till next day, when he died from the effects of the wound or neglect.

A very curious species of conveyance is used here by the Chinese. It is pushed, like a wheelbarrow, from behind, and goes on two wheels. A partition runs right down the middle, and on each side is a place for a passenger. When the wind is favourable, they actually put up a sail. Sometimes we saw a man on one side, and a woman on the other, and very frequently a Chinaman and his luggage.

One day we went to inspect one of the Baby Towers, of which there are numbers near Shanghae. They are wells surrounded by walls, with apertures through which the bodies are thrown in. It appears that all poor people's children, which die in infancy, are wrapped up in straw and deposited in one of these towers, to avoid the expense of coffins and burial ceremonies. They emit a terrible odour, and when the mass of straw bundles almost reaches the top of the tower, it is emptied, the contents are burnt, and the ashes spread as manure over the fields. Such a mode of disposing of the bodies of infants struck us as a great incentive to infanticide, a crime which is so very common in China.

I travelled with a lady, on one occasion, who had a Chinese wet-nurse, the father of whose child she told me it was her firm belief, from many circumstances, must have destroyed his offspring, and deposited it in one of these horrible places, or thrown it there alive; for the woman wept almost unceasingly, and refused to allege any reason for her constant grief.

We were told that it was not at all uncommon to dispose in this manner of female children, who are considered as only an additional burthen to be provided for, and an uncertain article of sale when they become marriageable; whereas boys are made to work as soon as possible, and thus, at an early age, become useful to their families.

According to a writer of note, the birth of a daughter is a matter of sorrow to the parents. "The best way," he goes on to state, "of satisfying the female babe is to furnish it with tiles to play with, whilst a boy is presented with gems and precious stones."

Such are the terms which he employs to denote the insignificance of the first, and the importance of the second. Although a very celebrated writer has computed that twenty boys are born to twenty-five girls, it is a well-ascertained fact that the male population is much larger than the female; facts which justify us in inferring that many female infants must be killed at their birth.

"One cannot reflect on this subject without shuddering. Infanticide is a crime of the most atrocious and heartless nature. The new-born babe has scarcely felt the caresses of its fond mother before it is drowned in warm water. At the very moment of its birth it is consigned, by a deed of darkness, to the grave. The excuse made for so horrible a crime is that instantaneous death is preferable to protracted misery—that the father is the best judge and arbiter of the destiny of his child.

"The government connives at this monstrous practice, because it acknowledges the sovereign authority of the parent over his offspring, makes him the arbiter of its destiny, allows the issue of life or death to remain in his hands, and considers female infanticide as the most effectual check upon the too rapid increase of population. Such principles could emanate only from that fallen spirit who was a murderer from the beginning. It is impossible to estimate the number of children thus inhumanly dispatched; but we can assure the reader, from actual observation, that the murder of female infants is a crime widely prevalent throughout the empire, and perpetrated with shameless atrocity."

CHAPTER VIII.

SET SAIL FOR JAPAN—ANECDOTES ON BOARD—VESSEL BECALMED—WEARY TIME—CAPE GOTTO IN SIGHT AT LAST—ENTRANCE TO NAGASAKI HARBOUR—LOVELY SCENERY—PAPPENBERG—ITS DISMAL TALE—PECULIAR SAIL—SLIGHT CLOTHING OF THE MEN—DESCRIPTION OF DRESS OF OFFICIALS—THE HARA KARI—OUR HOME—FLOWERS—STREETS OF NAGASAKI—VISIT TO THE TEA FIRING ESTABLISHMENT—SILK MERCERS—LACQUER WARE—PORCELAIN—PIC-NIC TO NAZUMISIMA.

CHAPTER VIII.

WE left Shanghae in a sailing vessel for Nagasaki, and, owing to an unfavourable wind and strong current, two days had elapsed before we reached the mouth of the Yangtsi. The first day we went on pretty well, soon getting clear of Gutzlaff Rocks, and steering straight for Japan.

Our captain was a native of Scotland, but having married in America, and his children settling there, he considered that his adopted country, and himself a naturalized Yankee. He was a kind-hearted individual, but had some peculiarities which often made us laugh. He was very loquacious, and, in the course of conversation, related to me how, being one day sent on business from his ship, he slipped on the snow at a corner of the street, and in his fall brought to the ground with him a young lady who happened to be near him at the time—fortunately, we must consider it, for, to make a long story short, she eventually became his bride. I found, subsequently, that the captain was in the habit of relating this story of his courting days to every new acquaintance.

He used to entertain us vastly with his remarks to the steward, a Chinaman, who, growing tired of a sea-faring life, had determined to return to his native land. For some reason or other, whether in obedience to the wishes of the captain, or from choice, I cannot say, he had cut off his tail and allowed the front part of his hair to grow, so that, except for the unmistakable Chinese stamp of feature, he might have passed for a native of any other nation. Now, however, that the thought of home was ever present to his mind, he had determined on allowing his hair to grow. At the time we became acquainted with him it had progressed considerably, but as it was not yet of a "tailable" length, it was always in the way, and looked more like the appendage of a wild animal than of a human being. This was a great source of annoyance to our captain, more especially as he had a lady passenger—namely, myself.

"Can't you cut your hair, steward?" he would say, pointing with the two middle fingers of his right hand to the undeveloped tail. "If I were you I would most assuredly try and be more like a civilized being, especially in the presence of a lady. Now, steward, I must beg, as a personal favour, that you will cut your hair."

To this, and similar remarks, made at every meal ten or eleven times, the meek steward never made a single reply, nor did he ever seem in the least inclined to grant the favour so graciously demanded. Sometimes in the middle of a repast, without saying anything to us, he would summon this indispensable attendant, and, as soon as he made his appearance, address him thus:

"Now, steward, you would oblige me if you would place the potatoes near the lady. Can you not see she is fond of potatoes? I wonder you have not the politeness to see that. Do try and be more observing and considerate—you will oblige me—I shall take it as a personal favour if you will observe these matters in future."

He would accompany these remarks with the usual action of his fingers, at the same time bending his head and body to and fro, as though to keep time to the words, and to add force to each syllable he uttered. The Chinaman's generally immoveable features would involuntarily relax into a species of semi-grin; and, though we strove to conceal our own inclination to smile, the very idea of a Chinaman's being polite, observing, or considerate, was too much for our risible muscles, and it was with the greatest difficulty we could refrain from laughing outright.

At last, after two days and nights spent in the river, we reached the boundless ocean, and, the first evening we were fairly out at sea, our captain came down to the saloon, his countenance expressive of unfeigned pleasure.

"This time to-morrow," he exclaimed, "with this wind, we shall be half-way to Nagasaki; and in three days from this I shall be proud to land you there."

This assurance gave us no little satisfaction, and we retired to our narrow couches with feelings akin to those of great glee. Unfortunately for us, however, the morning gave little promise of realizing the evening's prophecy. My nurse came to me, with a grave, inquiring look, and said, in her broken English,

"Ship no walkee, mem! Why ship no walkee, mem?"

I was, at first, at a loss to understand her meaning, but was not long in making the discovery that we were becalmed, the wind having sunk entirely over-night.

We continued thus for days, making little, if any, progress. To add to our discomforts, my husband, who had caught a bad cold from staying too late on deck whilst we were in the fog of the river, now suffered from a severe attack of bronchitis, which made our trial of patience all the more hard to bear. Our time of endurance was, indeed, a wretched and anxious one; and, no doubt, our own impatience made the ordeal appear even more lengthened and trying than it really was. But what benefit could we derive from murmuring against the will of Providence? If the delay was tedious, it had its compensations. The days were lovely, the sky cloudless, and the sea smooth as glass, with only the occasional sight of a shark, or smaller fish, to ruffle its tranquil surface. When night came the calmness was even more beautiful, each glittering star, in the vast expanse above, seeming mirrored in the depth below; but, alas! we lay like a log on the waters, our hearts longing for a breeze, but the wind lending a deaf ear to our wishes.

Fortunately, the captain was very kind-hearted and considerate, rendering us every assistance he could think of; and thus the time rolled on, till, in a week, a light breeze sprang up, wafting us slowly onward, lessening, by degrees, the four hundred and fifty miles which separate Japan from the mouth of the Yangtsi.

On the morning of the 23rd of May we first sighted land, the Gotto Islands, and, after rounding the Cape, also called Gotto, arrived in front of the Island of Fukaye, of which I took a small sketch. This is the largest of the group, all of which are in possession of the Japanese. As far as the eye could see, every part bore testimony to that careful cultivation by which land in Java is rendered so productive.

The night succeeding this day of hope was very foggy, and, as the sails were furled, we were compelled to a still further exercise of patience, and the vessel had to remain stationary till daylight. The longest night, however, has an end, and as, with the first glimpse of approaching dawn, all hands were busy, we were soon under weigh once more. Passing the fertile Islands of Iwosima and Takosima, a little further off to the right, we soon entered the narrow opening which was to lead us to our destination, and which we found it impossible to discover until close upon it.

The scene now grows more interesting each moment. Hemmed in by islands on one side, and by the mainland on the other, we passed quietly on, leisurely viewing everything that attracted our attention. Every inch of land seemed cultivated to the very summit of the highest hills. Except on the surface of the bare rock, every spot was green with vegetation. Numerous batteries are seen, like eagles' eyries, perched amidst the crags, the guns behind them mostly rusty from want of use.

The lovely Island of Pappenberg* next comes into view, its beautiful summit crowned with dark, luxuriant cedars, and its sides rising precipitous from the water, presenting little to the eye but rugged rocks, with occasional patches of trees and verdure. Here, we were told, a great number of those who had been converted to Christianity through the instrumentality of Xavier and other succeeding missionaries, were brutally murdered. So much has already been written on this melancholy subject, that few, if any, can be ignorant of the facts. Still, having witnessed the scenes hal-

---

* Pappenberg is supposed to be a name given to this island by the Dutch, as the Japanese call it Tacabuco.

lowed by the blood of these martyrs, a slight allusion to the circumstances of their death cannot be considered out of place.

The unfortunate victims were described to us as having been conveyed to the top,

> " Where the tall cedar rears its mournful head,"

and then ruthlessly thrown down, to dash against the rocks and stones below, and lie there, mangled, unsightly corpses, till the next receding wave swept away every vestige of blood and crime from the shore. How peaceful the scene looked as we glided quietly by! Contemplating the serene beauty of the landscape, who could divine that so " dismal a tale of woe " was inseparably connected with it?

A short distance from this there is another small island, Nazusima, not so hilly or rocky as Pappenberg, covered with trees, of bright, variegated foliage, and very picturesque.

We now approach Nagasaki, the long gulf, or inlet, leading to which, is nearly four miles long, though scarcely one mile broad in the widest part. Nagasaki is, perhaps, the most beautiful harbour I have ever seen, surpassing, I am even inclined to think, that of Singapore, with its myriad of emerald isles, in place of which we have here high towering cliffs, looking down upon scenes of woodland beauty, peaks rising so precipitously, it would seem as though they sprung from the verdant hills below.

Numbers of small bays present themselves on each side, as we sail past, with little boats moored to the shore. The latter are kept scrupulously clean, though unpainted. The sails they make use of are very singular, and somewhat picturesque, consisting, generally, of three stripes of sailcloth, or matting, united by a kind of lace-work, and thus forming one whole sail. It has a very pretty effect, and, I believe, serves the purpose better than any ordinary sail, for the men can unlace the connected parts, and take one or more in, when the increased violence of the wind, or a change in its direction, renders it necessary.

The boatmen are almost naked, and look most disgusting, for, unlike the Hindoo, they are by no means of a very dark complexion, their skin being almost as fair as that of the European; so that the exhibition of their forms appeared to us all the more glaring, lending no additional charm to the surrounding scene, but rather forming an eyesore one would gladly dispense with.

We arrived about noon, but as it was then too warm to go comfortably on shore, we stayed till the power of the sun had a little abated, amusing ourselves, in the meantime, with alternately watching novel sights on shore, and the amusing scenes of maritime life of which the ship in which we were passengers was the theatre.

As soon as the vessel was anchored the Japanese officials came on board, seemingly fearful of losing a moment in making the necessary inquiries.

One, who spoke pretty tolerable English, acted as interpreter for the rest, a second read aloud some questions in Japanese, which the other explained, and all the answers seemed perfectly satisfactory. Then after partaking of cake and wine, which, by the liberality of our captain, they were offered, and evidently thoroughly enjoyed, they very politely bowed and departed, leaving an officer on board, who was to remain during the time the vessel was anchored in the harbour.

There is a perceptible difference between the Chinaman and the Japanese. The contrast never strikes one so forcibly as on first arriving in Japan after leaving China. The people we have left behind are surly, impertinent, independent, self-sufficient, in their manner towards foreigners;

whilst those among whom we now are, poor and rich alike, have an innate politeness which is exceedingly pleasing, and address strangers in a respectful manner but rarely witnessed on the other side of the water.

All the officials wore the long flowing Japanese dress, which has some resemblance to a monk's garment. It is confined at the waist by a long band wound round the body, to which is suspended a case containing a pipe, tobacco-pouch, a singular kind of inkhorn, and the brush of which they make use in writing. Over this dress is worn a transparent, dark species of coat, upon the back and arms of which is a small, round, white mark, worn alike by all in whatever service they may be engaged, and denoting the person to whom they belong, or the employment which they follow.

On high days and holidays, all the officials wear a similar dress, of a light fawn or dove tint. Two swords are always stuck in their girdle as they walk about, but on sitting down they generally remove the longest, and place it at their side. With the smaller one they never part, as it is with this, or with the knife which is fastened on the scabbard of the weapon, that the "hara kari" is committed. The "hara kari" is the Japanese mode of suicide, generally resorted to on the discovery of any crime which would leave a stain on their honour, or a blemish on their fair name.

By thus escaping the hands of justice, the wife, family, and relations of the delinquent are regarded in no worse light than if he had died perfectly innocent. I have seen a native drawing of this mode of suicide, representing the self-sacrificing victim kneeling on the middle of a white cloth, his back resting on the small kind of stool which enables the Japanese to remain for hours in this posture. In his right hand is a drawn sword. He is looking upwards, as though invoking some deity. The people are assembled in vast numbers to witness the spectacle, such a suicide being regarded as a deed of great heroism.

"Mais revenons á nos moutons," as our neighbours across the Channel say; and I have no doubt you, kind reader, are as willing to hear of our quitting the vessel as we were to touch land again.

It was about six in the evening when the kind friend whose roof was to be our shelter came for us in his own boat. As the only means of ingress or egress was a ladder at the side of the vessel, an excessively inconvenient mode for ladies, I was obliged to submit to the process of being hoisted over the side in a chair, and then lowered into the boat.

We passed numbers of little Japanese craft on our way, mostly like those I have already described. All the boatmen seemed strong and sinewy, and, when not sailing their boats, scull them most vigorously, the passengers always sitting in the fore-part.

On gaining the landing-place, we prepared to disembark. Our feelings of joy and thankfulness, those only who have undergone ten days of doubt and uncertainty, and the same number of anxious, almost sleepless, nights, can fully enter into.

My husband, though evidently better, was still weak, requiring many little comforts procurable only on shore, and it was, therefore, with a lightened heart, and mind relieved of much anxiety, that I saw him mount the stone steps and reach the land.

Here, as in Shanghae, they have a kind of "Bund," though much narrower, cleaner, and quieter than the bustling Chinese one.

Our temporary home was a sweet sequestered nook situated on an elevated position, the natural beauty of which our host had certainly greatly enhanced. The house was a small, comfortable building, every interior door sliding backwards and forwards, instead of closing and opening in our ordinary way. Some portion of it, I was told, was formed of the wood of the camelia tree. Fancy this, ye lovers of flowers! Lovely flowers bloomed in the garden, and the flag-staff, which, as a consul, our host displayed, was erected in the centre of a miniature island, connected with the surrounding ground by small bridges, the water flowing beneath which was enlivened by numerous gold-fish. The scene before us had a pretty, rural aspect, and, on one side, we enjoyed a partial view of the harbour.

A day or two after our arrival we took a charming walk, passing through a shady wood, till we gained the summit of a small hill opposite the house, which we walked partially round, until we arrived at a spot commanding a magnificent peep of the Pappenberg and other smaller islands.

The most lovely flowers blooming here in wild luxuriance, I culled from " nature's bowers " a fragrant bouquet, which I carried triumphantly home. It consisted of so many varieties, several of them of great beauty, that a ball-room belle would have been proud to display it in her hand, and an English florist would have rejoiced to see such novel and profitable specimens blossoming together in his garden.

Among those flowers, the names of which were more or less familiar to me, were the sweet woodbine, the wild rose, the large sweet pea, azalia, seringa, orange blossom, and wax-like camelia, besides others which were quite new to me. The wax plant is a beautiful tree, growing in great abundance here. I picked a sprig of its bright green leaves, but, to my great annoyance, found it left dirty stains on my fingers, very sticky and difficult to remove, owing, I suppose, to matter oozing out.

We saw numbers of camelia trees, some twenty, some thirty feet high, I should suppose, with clusters of lovely flowers visible amidst their dark green foliage. This tree is likewise very common in China, but none of the specimens I saw there grow to such a height as those of Japan.

According to writers on this branch of Natural History, the camelia is so called in honour of Kamel, a Spanish Jesuit. They describe it as an evergreen shrub, frequently seen in China and Japan—one kind, called "Oleifera," furnishing the Chinese with quantities of oil, which they use for domestic purposes. Of the various kinds, the

Japonica, I believe, is considered the most beautiful.

During our stay in Japan we also frequently saw the lotus, which has a beautiful flower. The inhabitants make use of the root, when young, for food, and, when boiled, it is very tender and palatable. The flower, I believe, they regard with a kind of reverence.

The streets of Nagasaki are very numerous, and nearly all paved in the centre, which is slightly raised, with drains running down close to the houses on either side, so that they are very clean, and even after a heavy shower of rain soon become dry.

We were kindly taken to see a tea-firing establishment. In a large room numbers of women were seated at tables, sorting tea. They seemed quite surprised to see us, and rose *en masse* on our appearance. Coming towards where we were standing, they commenced at once a thorough investigation, one touching my hair, another my shawl, which, being of black lace, elicited many marks of approbation, testified by frequent exclamations of "ipioca, ipioca!" "good, good!"

The process of tea-firing in Japan is carried on after the Chinese principle, though the Japanese consider their tea of a much superior flavour. Whether it is so or not I am sure I cannot say, but certainly the European trade with Japan for it is generally admitted to be considerably on the increase.

We went next to a silk-mercer's, and were, as usual, conducted through the house; every visible part of which was as clean as if no one were allowed to touch its spotless walls, or tread its irreproachable floors, covered entirely with straw matting. Some women were engaged in domestic occupations, and, as we passed, looked up with a bright smile on their faces. Their hair is always dressed, for, when it is once done for the day, it is never let out of confinement until the next or the following morning.

We now entered a small court-yard, in which the Japanese taste for ornamentation was displayed in a very pleasing manner. We observed first a a small grass plot, in the centre of which tiny shrubs were planted. A little farther on was a miniature pond, where the gold-fish, in unmolested happiness, were swimming among the rocks and stones distributed about its moss-grown sides, variegated by beautiful ferns, arranged by a tasteful hand. Our progress in the yards was facilitated by planks put there expressly for the purpose.

Ascending a few steps, we then entered a little detached building, in the upper room of which we saw very delicate crapes, much cheaper than in China.

The shops of lacquer-ware proved places of great temptation, though we afterwards found that the articles purchased at Yokohama were of a much superior manufacture and more lasting quality, greatly excelling those produced in China, the gilding being brighter, the ornamental work better defined, and the finish more perfect.

As we were recommended to purchase porcelain in Nagasaki, where the finest articles of this description are manufactured, we made large investments in vases, plates, &c., &c., which, together with the egg-shell china cups and saucers, so transparent and delicate, form, now we are far from the land of the Tycoon, quite a valuable collection to us.

One day a pic-nic was proposed to Nazumi-sima, or Rat Island—*Nazumi* signifiying rat, and *sima*, island—situated not far from Pappenberg. We went in a large boat, towed by two smaller ones, manned with robust-looking Japanese. By some mistake our first steersman ran us against a junk, which, I believe, was slightly damaged, a *contretemps* from which, fortunately, nothing worse resulted.

The island is a lovely spot, though not so high and rocky as Pappenberg. We soon ascended the miniature hill, and wandered over the limited space at our command; visiting the spot where one of our countrymen has found his last earthly resting-place. A simple white cross was placed over the mound, but it has since been taken up, and deposited between two trees close by. As Japanese labourers frequent this island for wood, we may, without injustice, attribute this action to them, although it was doubtless done in ignorance, the object of the cross being, probably, as mysterious to them as the foreign inscription which was painted on it:—

W. CULLINGFORD, A.B.
H.M.S. " Spartan."
Oct. 3rd, 1855.

CHAPTER IX.

GENERAL VIEW OF NAGASAKI HARBOUR—THE IRON FOUNDRY—TEMPLE—PRIESTS—THEIR DRESS—JAPANESE CURIOSITY—"MAN'S TAIL"—JAPANESE WOMEN—THEIR DRESS—MEN'S MODE OF WEARING HAIR—IMMORALITY—VISIT TO A YACOONIN'S—WIFE'S DEVOTION—JAPANESE LADIES COME TO SEE US—THEIR POCKET-HANDKERCHIEFS—ARTICLES OF DOMESTIC USE—A FAMILY MEAL—INK HORN—PILLOW—OVERSHOE—STRAW SANDALS, &C.—JAPANESE MODE OF PUNISHING THOSE WHO OFFEND EUROPEANS—A FUNERAL PROCESSION—THE SIGNAL HILL—EXCURSION TO TOOKITS.

CHAPTER IX.

THE view of Nagasaki Harbour from the temple, which is situated on the side of the Compera Mountain, about a quarter of the way up, is very beautiful. The ascent to the summit, also, is very easy, and, had it not been for my husband's late illness, we should certainly have seen the bird's-eye view obtained from the top; but, as it was, he was not strong enough for the effort, and I did not care to go unaccompanied by him.

We contented ourselves, therefore, by inspecting the temple, and then, seated on a stone step, my husband took a sketch of the view, whilst I looked lazily on, and amused myself by watching the multitude assembled to gaze on us. It is a matter of surprise to me that I have never yet seen a sketch made from this point of view, for it is by far the most comprehensive.

The town lies at our feet, and the lovely harbour straight before us, the mountains on each side forming the boundary line against the clear blue sky. The white buildings on the side opposite to Nagasaki are called Hakonara. The iron-foundry established there is superintended by a Dutchman, and worked by Japanese.

We rowed across one morning to see it, and were astonished at the vast amount of European machinery made use of, showing how great is the desire for improvement, and, in spite of their suspicious fear of foreigners and foreign influence, their readiness to adopt really useful innovations.

The Compera temple contains images very similar to those worshipped by the Chinese. The priest's ordinary costume is not the simple grey habiliment used in China, but of a more elaborate description. We questioned a young priest as to the names of the various articles he wore, and I note down the following list, giving the names in Japanese and English: Waistband, *obee*; outer vestment, *kemono*; loose jacket, *how-odie*; under waistband, *c'tah obee*; loose inner vest, *jee-bung-nz*; stocking, *tabie*; sandals, *zodie*.

The priests make use of beads, and, we were told, are never married—points in which their religious system resembles that of the Roman Catholics.

We went to see some most exquisite azalias which were growing in one of the adjoining gardens, in which we seated ourselves awhile, to rest and look about us, affording the worthy people ample time for another good scrutiny of the foreign importation. One woman, touching my dress, felt the steel of the crinoline, and looking up to my face with a puzzled expression, said something in Japanese, which I interpreted, "What is that?" Her tone of astonishment evidently rousing the curiosity of others, an old priest, who stood near, also began to touch my dress, and, as he would probably have been followed by others, I was compelled to signify that the examination must end, not caring to go through the same ceremony with all.

In the principal temple we observed a curious-looking article suspended to the rails before the principal altar. On approaching close enough to examine the object of our curiosity, we found that it was the whole of the natural covering which a Japanese usually suffers to remain on his head. It had evidently either been cut off voluntarily by some self-accusing penitent, or some unfortunate delinquent had been deprived of it by others, as a mark of disgrace by which he would be distinguished until the new hair grew long enough once more to form the small tail.

On our return home we attracted the usual amount of attention, especially in passing through some of the more unfrequented streets, in which the people seemed much amused at seeing me take my husband's arm. One old man, catching hold of his good lady, who was nursing an infant, and, with dress disordered, exhibited a pretty fair portion of her person, placed her arm within his, endeavouring to walk as much as possible like us, to the undisguised merriment of the lookers-on, who burst into loud and prolonged shouts of laughter.

The Japanese women are, in general, much better-looking than the Chinese, the eye less elongated, and the whole expression of the face more open and free from cunning. There are many, however, whose faces proclaim their Chinese origin, the offspring, probably, of some of those intermarriages which occasionally take place. Their head-dresses and hair, which are objects of especial attention, are generally arranged after a very elaborate fashion, and when disposed to their entire satisfaction, are not disturbed again for a day or two.

The pillow of which they make use is admirably adapted for keeping the well-greased and pasted tresses in order. It is made of wood, and reminded us, at first sight, of a good-sized stereoscope. The head rests on a small roll of linen or paper, like a sausage in size, which they place at the top, and one would imagine that a stiff neck next morning must be the result of sleeping on such an unrefreshing pillow. As we are all, however, creatures of habit, they most probably prefer that to which they have always been accustomed.

The men, likewise, have their hair dressed only once in the twenty-four hours, and sometimes at longer intervals. A regular hair-dresser arranges their heads in the morning, invariably selecting the front part of the house, probably in order that the individual under his hands may be able to amuse himself by gazing at the passers-by during an operation so tedious and elaborate.

The entire top of the head, from the forehead, is always kept shaved, as clean as the face of a beardless boy. The rest of the hair, allowed to grow long, is saturated with grease, to which is added a kind of gum or paste, to make it stiff. The locks, thus bedaubed, are then combed up all round, and tied at the crown of the head, the ends sticking together forming a tail-piece, which is again doubled back and tied, plenty of gum being applied all the time, to make it pliable. When it is finished, it rests on the centre of the head, a short, neat little tail or knob.

The women dress very much like the men, with a loose, flowing robe, confined at the waist by a scarf. At the back they wear a bundle of cloth or silk, the most costly article of their whole attire. Every woman, whether of low or high degree, poor or wealthy, always turns round on passing another woman, and fixes her eyes on this singular appendage, a scrutiny which enables her to judge of the wearer's station and wealth. They redden their lips with a preparation the name of which is Bhen-tsu-ba. By means of another mixture, which many avail themselves of, they give them a golden tinge, the appearance of which strikes one, at first, as very singular.

The Japanese make companions of their wives in a more general sense than any Eastern nation I have seen or heard of, polygamy being, we were told, forbidden by law.

Every Japanese parent is allowed to sell his daughter to the proprietor of any "tea house," or other similar place; but only some of the poorer classes, I believe, avail themselves of this sad means of economizing their household, by parting with their offspring at the tender age of seven or eight. When they are thus sold, the better-looking naturally command the largest price. These poor children are, for their owner's own benefit, carefully tended, being kept in comparative seclusion until they attain the age of fourteen or fifteen, when they are compelled to commence an immoral course of life, the poor girls, like too many sad victims in our own land, being decked out in the gayest and most fanciful attire.

Either previous or subsequent to this time, any Japanese wanting a wife can purchase one of these young creatures, and be legally married to her; but if no such chance occurs, she is not permitted to leave the establishment until she is twenty-five, when she is perfectly free, and not in the least regarded as inferior to any other girl of her station in life—in fact, generally marrying well.

On one occasion, I remember, we visited the house of a Yacoonin, who received us with evident pleasure, treating us to tea and cake. After some minutes' conversation, his wife entered, accompanied by her female attendant. The officer introduced us to her, but as, unfortunately, she had not followed her husband's example in learning English, the remarks we exchanged were, as is almost always the the case when you need an interpreter, few in number. She was a good-looking young woman, thickly powdered, her eyebrows shaved entirely off, and her teeth blackened. The two last-mentioned operations are performed by every woman when she becomes a wife, and as they have generally strongly-marked eyebrows, and pretty regular teeth, with by no means small mouths, the disfiguring effect of the operations may be better imagined than described. The reason ascribed for this extraordinary practice is that each woman may show her husband that from henceforth she desires no admiration but his; though how a husband can reconcile himself to the disfigurement, I cannot think. Fancy wooing a lovely brunette, with hair like the raven's wing, and eyebrows to correspond, whose coral lips open to disclose two rows of pearls. Then, when the vows have been uttered, and this fair being becomes your own, picture to yourself what you must think on beholding the transformation that, in obedience to the tyrant custom, she has effected—the pearls suddenly turned to ebony, and the arch formed by the eyebrow now a bluish-looking desert!

After leaving this house, the friend who had accompanied us there informed us that the Yacoonin had fallen in love with his wife at a "tea house," and purchased her from the proprietor of the establishment.

Some Japanese ladies, during our stay, requested permission to come and see the "foreign lady." Accordingly, one lovely, warm day, they arrived, dressed in silks, the appendage at the back of the waist being orange or red in nearly every instance.

They brought some cakes for our little girl, with whom they seemed greatly delighted, carrying her about in their arms and stroking her hair, which, being very light, formed a marked contrast with their own dark locks. We offered them chairs, and for a few minutes they sat down, but evidently felt ill at ease, for they soon rose, walked about a little, and then squatted on the ground, where they felt more at home. Their tiny pipes were next produced, and, being filled with tobacco and lighted, were soon exhausted, for the bowl only holds sufficient for a good whiff or two. We gave them a glass of port wine, a beverage which had no charms for them, for they made wry faces, as though in pain, and stroked their throats to shew us the burning sensations it had produced. Our little child knocked one of the glasses over, and the contents being consequently spilt, they set to work to wipe it up with their pocket-handkerchiefs. The latter article is invariably composed of thin paper, cut into square pieces, and serving every requisite both of a pocket-handkerchief and table-napkin. As they are never without a dozen or two, they make use of a fresh one after each operation.

We were one day, by accident, witnesses to a singularly ludicrous spectacle. A man accosted us whilst we were walking down one of the principal streets, and requested to be allowed to shew us a dog he knew of, or possessed, as he had heard we were on the look out for a good one. Signifying our acquiescence, we turned and followed him through numerous by-lanes and alleys, till, at last, he stopped before a small, low building, and standing aside, invited us to enter. We did so without the slightest doubt or hesitation, little prepared for the absurdly indecent scene which awaited us within, causing us to beat a hasty retreat, and beg the man to bring the dog out if he meant to show it.

At the further end of the room we had so abruptly entered, was a portion partitioned off by a low wooden wall, within which enclosed space numbers of men and women were bathing *in puris naturalibus*. A thick vapour rose about them, and a strong sulphureous odour pervaded the place. They were dancing about as though half-mad. Whether this arose from sensations of joy or pain, I cannot say, but I know they reminded me forcibly of a representation of souls in purgatory I once saw outside a church in Antwerp.

I enjoyed several opportunities of observing the internal economy of a Japanese house. A small square table, about a foot high, with an outer edge of an inch deep all round, standing on four legs, is a common article of furniture. Upon this are generally placed five or six small cups, containing pickles of bamboo, ginger, &c., with sauces of various kinds; all very palatable to many European tastes, as well as Japanese. The family gathered and seated round this miniature table, not on chairs or benches, such luxuries being unknown and unappreciated, but on the mat which forms the floor-carpet, are then served by a

P

hard-working domestic, who seems a kind of maid-of-all-work, with rice, in small cups, from a steaming caldron.

The olive branches are generally squatted near, and, wherever we have seen the family meal, appear to have a propensity, probably heightened by keenness of appetite, for dipping their fingers into the pan (which the servant holds in one hand whilst she ladles out the rice), seldom meeting with any reproof. On one solitary occasion, however, the maid-of-all-work thought proper to show a little bit of authority. Placing the lid on the caldron, she put it once more on the fire, and then led the refractory urchins to their mother, on whose back slumbered the last-born, a fat, flabby-looking babe, supported by a long scarf slung across the left shoulder.

Of course no spoons are made use of to serve the various little delicacies that may be spread out. The chop-sticks, about half a size shorter than those used in China, dive in and out of the various little messes, bringing back the bit on which the owner has set his or her desire, whether a stew of chopped meat, the fish in the next dish, or any other choice morsel. They also eat a quantity of rice and fish. A particular kind of the latter they are fond of raw, and this they partake of with a vegetable like our radish, very finely scraped.

The Japanese wear a peculiar kind of overshoe, which, in wet or dirty weather, acts like a species of stilt to elevate them out of the mud. A sort of straw sandal is also very generally worn. The stocking is white, and made so as to show the shape of the great toe only, between which and the next there is an opening, so that the sandal when put on the foot fits exactly into this division, and thus remains immovable. Another sandal, made on the same principle, but more ornamental, is manufactured of wood, and intended for the use of the ladies, by whom it is worn as an overshoe.

I heard of one or two instances which go far towards proving that the Japanese are really very strict in punishing those who behave ill to Europeans, however some may doubt their inclination to do so. On one occasion a gentleman told us that, having a sick horse, he sent for a Japanese farrier, who undertook to cure it effectually, which in a few weeks' time he declared he had done. The gentleman, finding this statement incorrect, refused to pay until he was satisfied the horse was perfectly restored to health. It was in vain the man argued. As the owner of the animal was inexorable, the farrier was at length obliged to depart without the money he unjustly claimed. Before doing so, however, he visited the horse in his stable once more, for what reason the result will testify. He had not been long gone when the groom, with an expression of terror in his face, came running to his master.

"The horse is kicking," exclaimed he, almost breathless with haste and agitation, "the horse is kicking and jumping furiously—just as though it were mad!"

The master, on proceeding to the spot, found that the villainous farrier had, on his last visit, revengefully put chili seeds into the eyes of the poor brute, causing such intense pain as to occasion the furious fits by which the groom had been so startled. The gentleman immediately dispatched a messenger in search of the delinquent, who, on making his appearance, was charged with the brutal act; and his guilt admitting of no doubt, he was seized, well flogged, and securely locked up; immediately after which, the gentleman gave notice of the circumstance to the Japanese officials, sending them a detailed account of all particulars. The man, on being handed over to them, was tried and condemned to be decapitated, a sentence which was certainly unnecessarily rigorous, though he undoubtedly deserved severe chastisement for his barbarous and unmanly cruelty.

On another occasion a thief, having broken into a gentleman's house in Nagasaki, was caught in the act, and being likewise sentenced to decapitation, this fearful punishment was inflicted on him a day or two after.

Although such merciless severity cannot be commended, we hope it may prove a salutary lesson to his fellow-countrymen, who, when they are favoured with a chance, are only too ready to lay their hands on the property of others, and particularly of strangers, who they probably suppose may be plundered with greater impunity.

As we were passing along a street one day a singular-looking group arrested our attention. Two men in front carried gigantic artificial lilies, while another held a long stick, at the top of which was a large paper device, with various other articles, more or less curious. The most extraordinary was a kind of square framework, like a lidless box turned upside down, ornamented with white paper cut in scallops all round, so as to form a frill, and supported on four poles, one at each corner. We had only just completed our scrutiny of these objects when our attention was attracted to the house they were immediately in front of, from which was borne, on the shoulders of two stalwart-looking men, what looked to us exactly like such a barrel as Yarmouth bloaters are exported in. This we found on inquiry contained the mortal remains of an old woman of seventy-two, who, according to the invariable custom of the Japanese, was packed in a sitting posture within this circumscribed space, and thus conveyed to her last earthly home. The box-like construction which we had been inspecting having been placed over the barrel, as one covers eatables to keep flies off, the cortége moved on; four men dressed almost entirely in white closing the most singular funeral procession I have ever yet witnessed.

When we had been a little more than a fortnight in Nagasaki, we were looking forward most anxiously to the arrival of the steam-ship *St. Louis,* in which we hoped to secure a cabin for Yokohama, and for some days previous every signal gun we heard was supposed to announce her appearance. One day, whilst we were thus eagerly expecting her, we ascended the hill from which the Japanese signal any vessel in sight, and from the summit had a most expansive and lovely view of the entrance to the bay, with the islands of Pappenberg and Nazumisima immediately facing us.

Two houses, situated on two hills, constitute the look-out, the signal itself consisting merely of an old uprooted tree. This economical flagstaff lies on the ground when not required, and is placed upright when a ship is seen in the distance, on perceiving which in the town below, those on the watch immediately fire two guns.

Owing to the kindness of some gentlemen, residents in Nagasaki, who lent us ponies, we spent a delightful portion of one day in visiting a place called Tookits, about six miles distant.

We started between three and four in the afternoon, in a boat, and, after about half an hour's row, landed at a small creek, a little way up the bay. From this point we proceeded on foot through a village, to a spot where two chairs had been ordered to be in waiting for those ladies who, in consequence of the want of a side-saddle, were unable to ride, there being only one of these necessary conveniences for the use of three of us; the road, moreover, being rough and stony for a considerable distance.

After riding a short time in one of the chairs, I mounted the pony, thankful for the pleasant change. Passing through a narrow, rough road, we entered a stubble-field, now wending our way through lanes, then across numerous small ditches, or, more properly speaking, pools of water, and up and down flights of steps, a feat to which the animals seem to be well-trained, for as these flights of steps are constantly met with in the public road beyond Nagasaki, they necessarily become familiar with them. After a considerable amount of shaking, we reached a capital broad road, where we put our ponies to a good speed, and enjoyed a pleasant canter. The road, however, every now and then, was crossed by drains, covered over with raised flags, which might have proved inconvenient to horses unaccustomed to this curious impediment, but ours being evidently quite "up to it," took short leaps over each, without slackening their pace, or ever once stumbling.

When we passed any little hamlet on our route, which we did frequently, the inhabitants invariably came out to look at us, their faces lighted up with evident amusement, and their shouts of "O-hi-o! anata!" a kind of salutation, I believe, equivalent to our "How-d'ye-do?" following us as we rode along.

Some figures, on the right-hand side of the road, which were roughly hewn out on the face of a solid piece of rock, attracted our attention as objects of interest. They were six in number, resembling Buddhist images, and, I should think, very ancient, for their sharp edges were rounded by time, and the hollows filled up with weeds. This place, at some former period, had evidently been devoted to pagan worship, but is now neglected, and suffered to decay and crumble away.

We saw, to our left, about a mile from the village of Tookits, a curious rock, of great size and height, the shape of which particularly struck the beholder as most singular, to my fancy resembling exactly that of a child's doll, after it has been well battered, and deprived of the arms and legs.

After passing a troop of half-tamed ponies, kept by the poor people to carry goods, &c., we arrived at Tookits without meeting anything more worthy of remark. Galloping through the village, and on to the small jetty, or tongue, which is built out into the sea, the most lovely view it is possible to imagine lay before us like a panorama. Far in the distance a shadowy ridge of hills seemed to form a boundary-line between earth and sky; the sea appeared to be dotted with beautiful bright green islands and fairy-like rocks, whilst the hills behind, to all appearance, completely enclosed us, no place of egress being visible to our eyes.

The day was a lovely one, the air was calm, and the sea, with but a slight ripple on its surface, washed the shore of each little rock and island, its motion so gentle as to be almost imperceptible.

> "Scarce their foam the pebbles shook,
> But murmured meekly as the brook."

The villagers flocked out in numbers, and I verily believe, had there been a sick person amongst them, they would have found means to gain for him or her a sight of our cavalcade. They were very quiet and orderly, offering us no insult whatever. Many cried, "ipioca, ipioca," with similar ejaculations; and on my exclaiming, "saionara"—which is their good-bye—they seemed quite delighted.

This place is situated beyond the limit permitted to European excursions, and, according to the strict laws of the country, we had no right to venture so far. The gentlemen who accompanied us, however, having found it the best and indeed the only level road for riding near Nagasaki, broke the barrier of prohibition, out of "sheer necessity," and thus conferred a boon, not only on themselves, but also on visitors. At first the Japanese tried to oppose them, but their persistency soon overcame all the scruples of the authorities. No opposition is now offered to intruders, though, on our way back, we were followed by a short bi-sworded officer and two coolies, who allowed us, however, to go unmolested, and when we were clear beyond the boundary, retraced their steps to Tookits; there no doubt to report the result of their espionage to the head Yacoonin, an agent of the Prince of Satsuma.

On returning we met the same drove of ponies we passed before, and this time had some difficulty in getting by, for one kicked up at my horse, which started and reared, and nearly threw me into the paddy-field below. Luckily, however, I was saved the ducking in the mud which must have been the inevitable consequence of a fall there.

Dashing on, we were soon beyond kicking reach; and gaining the rest of our party, who were slowly advancing, I dismounted in order to allow another lady to ride to Tookits, for the day was fast declining, and it would have taken some time yet for the coolies to reach it with the chairs.

Having accidentally deviated into another route, some delay was occasioned, the party we had left not being able, on their return, to find out where we were. However, we all met, at last, at the village we had started from, where everything was arranged for our embarcation, and we were soon steering towards Nagasaki. There we partook of a very late dinner, and, after completing a hasty "packing," went on board the *St. Louis* considerably past midnight. At three in the morning we weighed anchor, and, steaming down the bay, were soon

> "O'er the glad waters of the dark blue sea,
> Our thoughts as boundless and our souls as free."

CHAPTER X.

PASSAGE TO YOKOHAMA—"SHIP NO WALKEE"—WE ENTER THE INLAND SEA—BEAUTIFUL NIGHTS—BAY OF YEDDO—FUSIYAMA—TOWN OF YOKOHAMA—FIRES IN THE NATIVE PART—COUNTRY ABOUT—EXCURSION TO KAMA-KURA AND BEYOND—RIDE—OUR FOOTMEN—TATTOOING—SINGULAR TEMPLE—STORY ATTACHED TO IT—HUGE BELL—DIFFICULTY IN DISCOVERING DIEBUTZU—FOUND AT LAST—RETURN TO KANAGAWA—LADIES HAIR-DRESSING GOING ON—DESCRIPTION OF IMPLEMENTS USED—MIRRORS.

CHAPTER X.

NEXT afternoon, about five, we passed the islands of Masima and Oogosima, the former on our left, both presenting the usual features of this part of Japan, bold overhanging cliffs and rugged rocks, all available portions of the land being carefully tended and cultivated. We obtained a glimpse of Sarado, another island, though it was partially enveloped in mist. Immediately before it was another small isle, on which we could see some fine large trees growing. Numbers of Japanese junks were sailing about, strange-looking boats, though by no means so heavy as those of the Chinese. As they are always kept scrupulously clean, they present a very neat appearance. Their plain wooden sides, with the exception of a narrow band of black or red about half-way down, are entirely innocent of paint. The land to our right was the large island of Kiusu, between which and us the Saksto Bana Islands, a pretty group, occasionally intervened, until, in consequence of the progress made by our steamer, they were entirely lost to sight.

We anchored that first night in Komoora Bay. The sea was smooth, and the surrounding view very fine. Near the beach we could occasionally distinguish several straggling villages. Behind us lay the broad expanse of boundless water, no land being visible in that direction; while before us, as well as to the right and left, were hills innumerable, besides the islands with which the sea was here and there dotted. One small mountain, the name of which is unknown to me, reminded us strongly, from the peculiarity of its form, of the volcano de Taal.

The following morning, about three o'clock, we had suffiicient daylight to resume our voyage. For three hours, I believe, we went on smoothly enough, but about six I was aroused by a rumbling, grating sound, similar to that I remember once before to have heard near Macao when the steamer struck, and I felt sure an accident of the same nature had happened now. After listening, however, for a little while, and catching no sound of any unusual commotion, I fell asleep again, convinced that if my suspicions were correct, no ill results could have been occasioned by the *contretemps*, or there certainly would have been more stir amongst the rest of the passengers.

I did not awake until near breakfast-time, when my ayah informed me that the "ship no walkee," which was equivalent to the news that "we were aground." Fortunately, the sea was pretty smooth, so that our vessel was not so much strained as it would have been had the weather proved boisterous, and the sea rough.

After our morning meal, we went to the foredeck, where, on looking over the side, we plainly discerned the reef on which we were fast. Our Japanese pilot afforded us great amusement by the contradictory accounts he gave to everybody who questioned him relative to this awkward mistake; the truth, without any doubt, being that, however learned he might be in other particulars, he was certainly ignorant of the existence of this rock. I really pitied the poor fellow, for he was evidently much annoyed by the unlucky circumstance. For fully five hours he remained in one position, apparently "wrapt in meditation," his arms crossed *à la Napoléon*, his brow contracted, and his small black eyes steadily fixed on the land before him. Our captain being a clever, active, and most indefatigable man, we felt that matters were as safe in his hands as, under existing circumstances, it was possible for them to be.

As the waters rose, hopes were entertained of getting off, and every gentleman on board lent a helping hand; but for some time all their exertions were vain, and it was not till about a quarter past one P.M. that their efforts were at last crowned with success, and we were once more afloat, to the joy of every individual on board, and steaming for the Bay of Wisinghacubie, nearly opposite the spot where our vessel had struck. There we anchored for the second night, leaving again by daybreak next morning.

As we rose from our berths, the vessel was passing in sight of some lovely scenery, to have a view of which, after a hasty toilette, we ascended on deck. We were then passing between the islands of Ongava, Matosima, Kakara, and Mindara, all cultivated and well wooded. At the foot of the hill in Matosima, we observed a very prettily situated village. The day was very fine, and the hours glided on pleasantly. At four P.M. we were very close to land, which we were told by the pilot was the island of Oohsima, forming part of the Prince, or Damio, of Skuzen's territory. Behind us was Oronosima, a small but exceedingly pretty isle.

About this time the ever-watchful eye of our captain, now more vigilant than ever, after the mishap occasioned by the ignorance of the pilot, discovered another small rock, some distance ahead, only perceptible by the foam of the waters breaking over it. The chief officer immediately took the bearings, and reported it as being only half-a-mile off, Oronosima being W.N.W. ¼ W.; Oohsima N.E. by N.; and this newly-discovered reef, E.S.E. ¼ E.

About midnight we entered the Straits of Simonosaki, greatly to our disappointment, for we had retired already under the impression that we should not have progressed so far on our voyage for some hours later. Those who sat up described the scene as beautiful, the night being clear, and the moon shining brightly. Fortunately, however, our missing it was of little consequence, for we saw it to perfection on our return, as my readers will find described further on.

The day broke, as usual of late, in unclouded splendour. We were now in the Suonada, or inland sea, which, in fact, as we continued our sail over its transparent waters, resembled a "succession of lovely lakes," one opening into the other. When the vessel was in the centre of one of these, no outlet was visible, the land on each side consisting of islands so closely grouped together as often, from a distance, to present the appearance of one unbroken shore. From the stern we could discern the opening by which we entered, now dwindled in the distance almost to a needle's point, whilst the hills before us, apparently united, seemed to leave no visible means of egress.

On approaching nearer, we discovered a narrow strait, through which we passed, the land towering high on each side. In a few minutes we gained the other side, to find ourselves once more in a large lake. Fortunately for us the moon was at its full, and the nights consequently were most lovely. As the weather was so fine, we never anchored again during the voyage, so that it was quite a delightful excursion to all.

The evening of the 9th of June was especially beautiful. We were approaching Nivarra, where we were told our steamer had anchored on her last trip. The land on all sides appeared to be so close to us, that we seemed to be threading our way for hours through a maze of shadowy islands. It was a still, calm evening, " clothed with the moon and silence." The calm expanse of water, undisturbed even by a single ripple, was like a mirror in which the few lights visible from the shore appeared reflected. A scene of more entrancing beauty could not be imagined, some of these lights being perched like eagle's eyries amid the crags, while others close to the water's edge, to my fancy, resembled with their reflection long gilt spears with jewelled tips. Was it not a shame to grow drowsy mid scenes like these? In vain we wrestled with Nature's hint that it was time to seek her soft restorer, balmy sleep. The very enchantment of the scene, as we sat on deck contemplating it, seemed gradually to steep our senses in forgetfulness. We endeavoured, by walking up and down, to resist the powerful call of " tired Nature;" but it was of no avail, and at last we were reluctantly compelled to obey her dictate, and descend to our dormitories.

Next morning, we passed very near the mansion or castle of a Damio, an ugly-looking pile close to the beach, consisting, as far as we could discern, of a house surrounded by high walls.

About mid-day we neared the island of Avasisima, large, well-wooded, and hilly. The current now began to run very strong, and as the wind was unfavourable, we were unable to proceed at a rapid rate.

June 11.—I woke early, perhaps in consequence of the uneasy motion of the vessel, now so perceptible after the long calm, for about four A.M. we had passed through the Kino Channel, bid adieu to the inland sea, and were now rolling and tossing in the Pacific Ocean. This we were told by the chief officer, who further informed us that the land visible to our left was the island of Nipon. Many of our fellow-passengers absented themselves from this day's dinner, preferring, whilst the vessel rolled and pitched so much, a recumbent to a sedentary position.

By next morning we had entirely lost sight of land. The wind was blowing right ahead, and we were obliged to steer three points out of our course; but about noon a favourable change took place, and we were thus enabled to make straight for our destination. Ere the sun set, land being again distinguished, our captain was able to assure us that, in all human probability, we should reach Yokohama early the following day. With this pleasant piece of information we retired, awakening at dawn to find ourselves in the Bay of Yeddo.

FUSIYAMA.

About eight we were on a line with Vries Island, in which is an active volcano, sending forth continuous volumes of smoke.

Fusiyama, rising in a cone-like form, next became for a short time visible, its summit crowned with pure snow, contrasting with the dark colour of the rocks in the lower parts.

The mountain itself is first seen in faint black streaks, which gradually widen, till, the lines of snow growing small and fine, it is at last revealed in all its naked majesty. Though I have seen numerous perpetual snow-capt mountains in Switzerland, the Pyrenees, &c., I have never witnessed one presenting, in this point of view, an appearance so remarkable and so curious.

In most cases when the snow melts off, it does so in patches, but here, probably owing to the shape of the mountain, it looks as if portions had been designedly removed in such a way as to leave the white stripes perfect and unbroken, in their course down the sides, yet it is far from presenting anything like a stiff or formal appearance, the lines from a distance seeming to graduate, so as to form a soft and harmonious whole. As the hills beside this object of interest and beauty are small and insignificant in comparison, it stands almost, we may say, alone in its solitary grandeur.

This mountain, as may be presumed from the designs of it which are constantly seen on the lacquer ware, porcelain, &c., is greatly admired by the Japanese. It derives its name, we were told, from *Fusi*, matchless, and *Yama*, mountain, the Matchless Mountain, and is said to be nearly fifteen thousand feet in altitude.

About noon we were just off Perry Island, so named from Commodore Perry, though what the native name is I know not. At half-past one P.M. we anchored in the harbour of Yokohama, the town of that name being close by to our right, whilst on the opposite side of the bay is the town of Kanagawa.

In 1861, about a year before our visit, great part of the Japanese houses in Yokohama were destroyed by fire; and now again, six weeks previous to our arrival, a second conflagration has laid waste all that remained from the first—fortunately, however, leaving the newly-constructed houses uninjured.

The Japanese domiciles, being constructed entirely of wood, are speedily consumed, whilst, on the other hand, owing to their simplicity, they are very quickly and easily re-constructed; and as the Japanese lose as little time as possible in bewailing a misfortune, they soon set themselves actively to work, with the view of repairing the loss they had sustained, so that, on our arrival, we did not see the place in such an utter state of desolation as we had been led to expect we should.

The small pier at which we landed is a good solid-looking piece of masonry, but was not quite completed. To the left of it they were making a Bund, similar to those in Shanghae and Nagasaki. In this quarter we find the European settlement, consisting of numbers of houses, now inhabited, and others rapidly rising up, which extend as far as the creek where the Bund, when finished, will terminate. On the opposite side is a hill on which a house for the British Minister is to be erected. The space for it is already enclosed, near the edge of the cliff, from which the view of the bay is very fine. When completed, it will be a delightful summer residence, but the situation must be a bleak one in winter.

On leaving the boat we first proceeded to the Custom-house, which is a little to the left of the pier I before mentioned. Here we had our luggage examined, the quantity, however, proving too small to require minute or lengthened inspection.

The Japanese part of the town lies to the right of the pier. The gates in the streets, as is usual in all towns of this singular country, are situated about a quarter of a mile apart, or less. In case of a disturbance, they are immediately closed, thus precluding all possibility of the inhabitants assembling together in great numbers.

I was surprised to find that every European here has wooden palisades round his compound, or grounds attached to the house, which, in case of any sudden attack, serve as a temporary defence. Though this is no doubt a very prudent precaution, it is by no means an ornamental addition to their property.

Behind the settlement there is a flat piece of ground, apparently waste land, which we were informed is to be the race-course, though, like many other projects here, it is evidently as yet only in its early infancy. During our stay we took many walks in different directions, and observed that the country around and beyond is very pretty, being well wooded and hilly.

One day we made a long excursion by sea and land. We left Yokohama in a boat at a very early hour of the morning, and, as a capital breeze was luckily blowing in our favour, it filled the sail of our craft, and made it skim at a delightful rate over the water. The sail was made in the usual manner, of three distinct pieces of matting attached to a yard, and hoisted almost to the top of the mast. We were soon passing Treaty Point, so named from the fact that the vessels were lying off it when the treaty with America was signed, after which we skirted along Mississippi Bay.* All this part of the country is excessively pretty, and the day being fine, we felt quite exhilarated with the sail.

In less than half an hour we arrived opposite a beautiful island, known to Europeans as Webster's Island. Here the rocks present a most curious appearance, in some parts quite resembling a rough castellated wall. One side of the island, indeed, looked like an old castle, with two projections resembling watch-towers, the hollow between being covered with different kinds of moss and ferns of various shades—

> " The wild rocks shaped as they had turrets been,
> In mockery of man's art."

* Mississippi Bay, so called from the name of the ship in which Commodore Perry came to Japan, and which anchored here in 1852.

Further on we entered a small river, where the sail was lowered, and the men began to use their sculls most vigorously. To our right, on a pebbly beach, numbers of fishermen were employed repairing their nets, women and children were scattered here and there engaged in various occupations, a lovely hill behind forming a charming background to this picturesque tableau. On the left side of the river were beautiful overhanging cliffs, some of which were similar to those we had already seen on Webster's Island.

Here, with but a slight stretch of fancy, I could distinctly trace the ruined remains of some ancient castle, with its chapel attached, a portion of the Gothic window of which seemed left by time to show what had been its "light of other days." Thus can imagination, inspired by the contemplation of nature, reconstruct the creations of the past, give form and substance to its own poetic conception, and invest with an appearance of reality the beautiful dreams in which it loves to indulge.

After about twenty minutes' or half an hour's sculling, we reached the village of Kanazawa, where, on entering the principal hotel, we gave orders that a repast should be in readiness for us on our return. We then left the house to inspect the horses, which some friends had kindly promised should await our coming.

Although the Japanese, as I suppose all know, invariably make use of straw shoes for their horses, those sent for us were less economically, but more substantially, provided with protectors to their hoofs, in the shape of the regular iron shoe. We were accompanied by no fewer than three grooms, who acted also as guides; for the road we were about to take is seldom frequented by Europeans, and the friend who came with us felt uncertain of being able to find the route. These three unfortunate beings had to keep up with the pace of our animals, whether at a gallop or a walk; and I must say they performed this feat as if they were well accustomed to it.

I amused myself vastly with contemplating the back of the groom who sometimes preceded my horse, for it was really a study. Perhaps the reader may smile; but let him restrain the excitation of his risible muscles until he has heard the explanation which I have to give. A most elaborate subject, most cleverly tatooed, was what occupied my attention. It represented a Japanese, in full dress, seated in an arbour, as I judged by the profusion of red and blue flowers that appeared in all directions. He was playing the flute, the harmonious sounds of which were apparently exciting the admiration and delight of two ladies, who, with an immense number of pins in their hair, and dressed in the height of Japanese fashion, were standing near. We observed that this process of tatooing is very common about here. It is generally confined to the back, but not unfrequently extends the whole length of each arm, sometimes even embracing great part of the chest. The designs are of great variety—some purely floral, others including the bodies of dragons, snakes, &c.

A short distance from the village of Kanazawa, our route lying through an undulating country, the scenery begins to grow charming. The road is sometimes cut out of solid rock, not presenting the gloom of a tunnel, but open to the sky. Lovely ferns and tiny shrubs luxuriate in all directions, and large trees form a natural arch above. In some parts of the rock we found niches hollowed out, in which were figures roughly hewn in relief.

An hour's ride brought us to Kama-kura, a place which we were informed was the capital of the whole empire six hundred years ago. It looks merely a straggling village now, but in some of the houses still left, and in the numerous temples grouped together, we find relics of its former greatness. The latter, nine in number, extend over about twelve acres. Six are built on the level ground, and the other three on an eminence, to which we ascend by a very long flight of steps. Like the temple of Janus in the days of Rome's pride and glory, one of them, of a circular form, which is said to be a thousand years old, is kept closed during the time of peace, and open in case of war at home or abroad.

A singular road runs through this place, the centre part being raised some feet above the sides, from which it is separated by grass-covered mounds, about half a yard in height, with openings at regular intervals for people to enter. The raised part seems to have been specially set apart for members of the Japanese court, or for natives of rank and station alone; the more ordinary individuals walking on the side paths—one of the many proofs of the great distinction made between patrician and plebeian in Japan. How far this system of distinction still continues we were unable to ascertain; but, as this road now presents a somewhat neglected appearance, it was evidently more used when Kama-kura was in the height of its power as a capital and a city of importance.

Our friend was most anxious to shew us a huge figure of bronze he had himself once seen, but which no European had been allowed to inspect until 1861, a year previous to our visit. As he had, unfortunately, forgotten the locality, we spent much time wandering about in a useless search for it. Deceived by some one whose advice we followed, we entered a village which we were led to believe no European had ever yet seen, where we visited a most curious temple. An old man, with a few grey hairs gathered into a tiny knob on the summit of his cranium, seeing we were strangers, and feeling anxious, no doubt, to relieve our pockets of some of the weight in coin they contained, signified his wish to show us this singular place.

Having accepted his offer of guidance, we followed his feeble footsteps, and proceeded to the temple, which we found to consist of three good-sized caves excavated out of the solid rock. Ascending to these by a flight of steps, we entered the first, which was entirely surrounded by small figures, one, much larger than the rest, being placed conspicuously in the centre. The old man was very anxious for us to stand on a circular spot in the floor, exactly opposite this figure, which we at first refused to do, suspecting he wished us to make obeisance to the idol. Finding, however, this was not his desire, we afterwards complied with his wish, to the undisguised delight of our ancient guide, going through the same mysterious ceremony in all the caves.

Though we could make out most of what he said, we could not comprehend his reason for this curious proceeding, our friend who kindly acted as interpreter being unable to understand his explanation, which he considered to be owing to the fact that we were in a village the inhabitants of which had never been accustomed to speak to Europeans in their native tongue, those who have frequent intercourse with foreigners usually adapting their language to the comprehension of those they speak to, and thus naturally falling into a slower and more distinct mode of articulation.

Being however too curious to be baffled by trifles, we requested our friend to try his utmost to ascertain what could be the old man's reason for his singular entreaty, and our perseverance was subsequently crowned with success. It appears that in each of these caves, below the circular spot on which the old man wished us to stand, there is an excavation, in which, some time ago,

R

three men were buried alive for refusing to worship after the manner of the Japanese; and now it is the earnest desire of every bigot of their creed to persuade all who enter the temple to stand directly above these tombs—an act which, in their opinion, is probably significant of their trampling on the dust of the heretics buried below. Had we known this at the time, how reluctant we should have felt to comply with such a revengeful request!—with what a deep feeling of interest we should have regarded the stone which covers the honoured bones of those conscientious martyrs who suffered death in a living tomb rather than render to idols of wood and stone the worship which is due only to the living God! Who knows but these three formed part of the band of Christians once so numerous in Japan? The story of these caves may be the sequel to the gloomy tragedy of Simambarra and Pappenberg.

On descending from this place, the old man led us to a temple situated on a very high hill, up to which we toiled, in the heat of the sun, by a long flight of narrow steps. When we reached the summit we discovered an object of curiosity in the shape of an immense bell suspended from a kind of wooden shed, and struck in the usual manner on the side, by a long thick pole which was attached by chains to the rafters above. This pole, an uncouth-looking piece of machinery, is pulled backwards by the exercise of considerable strength, and, in its rebound, hits the bell with great force, producing a very loud, long, continuous, and not unfrequently re-echoing sound. We purchased one of the pictures representing it, which are sold on the spot. From the characters around, it appears that it was put up in commemoration of some great event in the annals of Japanese history. In the temple near this huge bell, which very much resembles other buildings of the same nature we have seen and described, there was nothing remarkable, the only point in which they differ from each other being the variety of their images.

We rested on the steps of the temple and partook of a little refreshment, offering some champagne to our old guide, which he drank with apparent gusto, receiving, with evident pleasure, at the conclusion of our repast, the empty bottle, an article which, to our great surprise, the Japanese seem to value very much. During our voyage through the inland sea, boats frequently came alongside for the express purpose of obtaining empty bottles, which the passengers amused themselves by throwing into the water, in order to see the boatmen plunging and diving for them, a feat which, in their almost nude state, is not attended with the subsequent inconvenience of wet clothes. I remember one day I threw a very pretty scent-bottle, thinking how highly they would value it as a rarity, but to my great annoyance, and their undisguised disappointment, owing to my stupidity in forgetting to cork it, it filled with water and sank before one of them could reach it.

We now retraced our steps, mounted our patient steeds, and set off anew in search of the large bronze figure. As everybody we questioned seemed ignorant of its whereabouts, we could gain no information respecting it. In the hope of meeting with better success we changed our route, and went fully a mile or two in another direction, when, finding ourselves once more on the wrong track, we returned to Kama-kura, and with some difficulty procured a boy to act as guide, under whose direction, after a ride of a good mile or more, we at last found what we had so long been in quest of.

Dismounting, and leaving our horses in charge of the tatooed grooms, we walked up the long avenue before us, at the end of which was the large figure, a photograph of which was taken on the spot by an American gentleman. Its great size was rendered more apparent by comparison with the diminutive appearance of the human beings who stood beside it. My husband and myself mounted upon the wall which forms its pedestal, and from thence scrambled up the folds of the dress, and seated ourselves on the thumbs of the two hands. As it was a temple, we determined on seeing the interior. Entering, accordingly, by a low door, we found ourselves in a good-sized room, lit by two small windows let into the back of the figure. The air within was stifling, for it was mid-day, and the sun shone with its full power on the bronze, which felt quite hot to the touch. This huge image, whose height is fifty Japanese feet, which I am told is equal to half as many more English ones, was made all in patchwork, the pieces being joined together by a kind of soldering process, the execution of which is so perfect that the joins are not perceptible on the exterior. We could distinguish the form of the figure inside the temple, the head forming an extreme point for the top or roof. After some few minutes' conversation with the man who acted as guide, and purchasing a native portrait of the revered object, from which, I am sorry to say for the artist, no one could possibly obtain any correct impression of it, we bade adieu to Diebutzu, and returned to the village of Kanagawa.

On riding up to the hotel we found that there had been a great influx of visitors, and were not long in discovering that a hairdresser was busily engaged exercising her functions on the heads of the ladies present. Though I was very tired, and my appetite uncommonly ravenous, I could not resist a desire to linger awhile at the doorway and watch this public operation. It was fortunate I did so, for I witnessed two different styles of hair-dressing, both equally elaborate and laborious, and made an exact memorandum of the various articles used during the whole process. We counted no fewer than twenty-eight small combs, numbers of lengths of black thread, white ditto, black grease (made use of in order not to shew amid the jetty tresses), a thick kind of waxy-looking grease, applied in order to make the hair stiff, and thus more subservient to the will of the operator. Besides these were endless quantities of wire shapes, pads, and papers cut to sizes, all of which were in constant requisition.

The Japanese women have no parting in the centre, but a piece of hair immediately in front is divided off an inch and a half in breadth, the divisions on each side of this lock joining in the middle of the head, about half a finger length from the forehead. The hair for a small space behind this is always kept shaved, the front piece being tied immediately above the shaved part, and generally joined in with the back, though it is sometimes cut quite short after it is tied.

The hair at the back and sides is suffered to grow very long, separated off, then tied, and some portions dressed, all the rest being re-united and again divided, rolled over pads, round shapes, &c., in a manner too intricate to admit of any intelligible attempt at explanation. The mode most generally adopted, probably from being the least elaborate of all I saw, consists of a large bunch of hair on the crown of the head, the front dressed as usual, leaving but little hair immediately at the back. This bunch they decorate according to their means, station, or the toilette the occasion requires, invariably with some ornament or other, not unfrequently consisting of pins and beads, arranged in quite as inexplicable a manner as the head gear of the Chinese ladies. The mirrors they make use of are very primitive, made, not of glass, but of metal, polished bright as silver, the reverse side being ornamented with storks, flowers, and leaves in an artistic style.

CHAPTER XI.

OUR RETURN TO YOKOHAMA—SALT DRYING AND BOILING—WEASELS AND RATS—JAPANESE HOUSES—WANT OF CHIMNEY—SLIDING DOORS AND WINDOWS—FIRE HOUSES—FANS—EARTHQUAKES—JAPANESE ACCOMPANIMENTS TO A GIFT—KANAGAWA—THE NORIMONS—JAPANESE MODE OF ANNOUNCING THE NAMES OF THEIR VISITORS—OUR DISAPPOINTMENT—WE LEAVE YOKOHAMA—BAD WEATHER—CONTRETEMPS—FORTUNATE ESCAPE IN THE STRAITS OF SIMONOSAKI—STRAITS OF HERADO—ARRIVAL AT NAGASAKI—RECEPTION THERE — VISIT TO A MERCHANT'S HOUSE — COOL REQUEST OF HIS WIFE—YACOONIN'S IMPRESSION OF HIS OWN MUSICAL TALENTS—JAPANESE THEATRE—KIND OFFER.

CHAPTER XI.

WE only stayed at the hotel time enough to have something to eat, and then left, walking for a considerable distance, as, in consequence of the ebb of the tide, our boat lay some way down the river.

We passed several marshes and reservoirs for salt, which appeared to me, from the information I obtained, and the hasty inspection which was all I was able to bestow, to be deep pits, dug in the bed of the marsh at equal distances from each other. When it is full tide these swamps are completely covered, and the gates of the reservoirs being closed at the fall, the saline matter is deposited in the pits abovementioned, which are sheltered with barrel-like boxes, to protect them from rain. It is then taken to the factories, where it is boiled and re-boiled, dried in the open air and in ovens or pans, and then sold either in lumps or in a pulverized state.

We entered one house where the salt was boiling in a large trough, and tasted some which had already undergone the process.

On gaining our little craft, the crowd, which had been gradually collecting, grew very large, the inhabitants of all the villages in the neighbourhood having apparently turned out.

> " The tidings spread, and gathering grew the crowd;
> The hum of voices and the laughter loud."

We stepped into the boat, and left amid the universal cry of *sion-ara*, which followed us till it grew faint, and then was lost in the stillness of a lovely evening, for the wind had sunk, and not a murmur was heard save the slight sound caused by the sculling, and the boat cutting its way through the waters. In spite of our fatigue we intensely enjoyed the serene beauty of the scene. The dying beams of the sun, which was just setting as we reached the open sea, gilded the rocks of each small islet with golden light, and were reflected with the calm splendour of evening in the rippling waves below. We did not arrive at Yokohama till late, and glad we were to reach the house of our friend, which, during our stay, afforded us so hospitable a shelter.

We used to be amused by the repeated pattering of little feet overhead, occasioned, as it afterwards appeared, by rats, which abound here in such numbers that scarcely a house is free from them. To hunt down these nuisances, weasels regularly establish themselves on every roof, reminding one of the lines in De la Fontaine's Fables:

> "La nation des belettes,
> Non plus que celle des chats,
> Ne veut aucun bien aux rats."

> "The weasels live, no more than cats,
> On terms of friendship with the rats."

The houses, as I have observed before, are very slightly built, mostly of wood, many of the poorer ones being composed only of a light bamboo framework, covered with thick mud, which when dry receives a coat of plaster—thus assuming, when completed, a solidity of appearance that anyone who had seen the building in its early stage of erection would scarcely have expected. The roof is generally made of a kind of tile, often arranged in alternate stripes of brown and white, or black and white, the eaves drooping over the house sides to protect them from sun or rain. As I do not remember to have seen, except in the European dwellings, a single chimney, I cannot imagine how the smoke escapes when it is damp or cold, and the inhabitants are obliged to close their doors and windows.

The doors and windows, and almost everything here, seemed invariably to go on slides. At night the closing of all the wooden screens outside the verandah (considered an important business for the protection of the house) is an operation that lasts fully five minutes.

Every village, I believe, throughout the whole kingdom of Japan, contains one or more fire-proof houses, and in each town there are numbers of them. The walls of these buildings are very thick, the roof is formed of earthen tiles, and the windows generally of wood sheathed in iron, which they cover with a thick coating of mud. Into these houses, in case of fire, the people stow their effects, thus protecting them alike from the raging element and from the prowling thief.

The Japanese, like the Chinese, make great

use of the fan, the rank and station of each individual being determined frequently by the style of this article, or the design painted upon it.

At Kanagawa and Yokohama earthquakes occur very frequently, sometimes, I am told, as often as once a fortnight. Whether these have any connection with the adjacent "Matchless Mountain," or not, is a point upon which I have heard much disputation, but no decisive conclusion has ever been arrived at.

During the time we were with our host he received, according to a curious custom of the Japanese, a present by which they indicate the superstitious reverence with which they regard the memory of their ancestors. Whenever a gift is made by them, a dried shell-fish, called *awabie*, together with a bit of sea-weed, is attached to the paper in which it is enclosed; the reason they assign for this being that the founders of the Japanese kingdom, or the first settlers on the principal island, were fishermen. The observance of this practice is, therefore, looked upon as an imperative duty, by which they remind themselves of the ancestors from whom they derive their origin, and whom, like the Chinese, they regard with the utmost respect and reverence. Whether they worship them or not, I cannot exactly say.

I have a picture from a native painting, representing a procession on the grand feast-day, in honour of these departed friends and relatives. Once a year this festival is held, corresponding, I fancy, with the Chinese feast of lanterns, both taking place sometime during the month of August.

Kanagawa is on the high road to Yeddo. In fact, the road which bisects the town is part of the main route running throughout the whole empire. We rowed across the bay to see it, purposing to return by the road, as there is a very pretty path through some lanes and nicely wooded country from Yokohama; but time did not admit of this, and we were therefore obliged to take to the boat again, after we had seen all the sights of the old town.

The shops are very poor, and the whole place is far from presenting the neat appearance of Yokohama. Whether this is owing to its being on the high road, and the constant traffic consequent on this, or not, is doubtful; but, from its being much more crowded and bustling, it is not unlikely. There are a number of hotels, and hostelries containing ponies of various sizes, also buildings expressly for Norimons, the favourite Japanese conveyance, resembling a rabbit hutch more than a chair or carriage. These are carried in the same manner as the Chinese sedan, by two men. The interior is a small confined space, in which you are compelled to sit in an extremely uncomfortable position.

There is one peculiarity in the Japanese hotels which struck us as very curious—namely, the custom of inscribing, on the door-post outside, the name of every visitor; in order, I concluded, to inform inquirers for parties supposed to be lodging there.

We saw a great many Yacoonins, and other officials and travellers, *en route* for the capital. Some were mounted on spare-looking beasts, proceeding at a remarkably slow pace, a groom invariably leading the horse. Their luggage followed in the rear, swung on a thick bamboo pole, which the coolies carried on their shoulders. Others, again, were stowed away into the odd-looking Norimons I have described before, whilst a few of the poorer brethren made use of their legs, proceeding nearly as fast as those who were conveyed.

We were very much disappointed in not being able to visit the capital during our stay in Japan; but all our efforts to go there proved vain, owing to unforeseen circumstances, together with the shortness of our sojourn in the vicinity. Our Minister at Yeddo was dangerously ill, which precluded the possibility of his receiving us at his own house. Before we had his decisive reply to the request we made through the Consul (then resident at Yokohama) some days had elapsed, leaving our remaining ones very few in number; for, though the distance was less than twenty miles, the cooly sent with the message took three days to go and return.

We next asked the Consul if any objection would be raised to our going to Yeddo under the protection of the Minister of another power, to which he politely answered none. We adopted this precaution to avoid all possibility of any subsequent unpleasantness, as some travellers, on being refused, for reasons best known to the parties, have gone by the permission of others, and, in one case, were ordered back by the English Minister then officiating in Japan. Our case was different, as it was wholly owing to Colonel Neal's severe indisposition.

We applied next to the American Consul, who so fully entered into our disappointment, that, could he have succeeded for us, I felt sure he would. Three days of anxious expectation passed by, when we received the answer to our second application, which was to the effect that the American Minister had at present no more accommodation for visitors, for his house, being only a temporary one, was small, but in two or three days he would be most happy to receive us. Unfortunately our steamer sailed before the expiration of this time, and, as we strained our eyes longingly in the direction of Yeddo, where, on a fine clear day, the forts are just distinguishable, we could only give a sigh of regret, and exclaim, in the words of a well-known song—

"Thou art so near, and yet so far."

We had now, on our return, very unpleasant weather. It was very rough as soon as we entered the Pacific, the winds, which were contrary, frequently coming in gusts, with torrents of drenching rain. For three days the vessel knocked about, unable to enter the narrow passage leading to the Suonada Sea. On the morning of the fourth day the sea became calmer, and we entered the Kino Channel, passing the village of Kimo-saki, situated in the hollow of a conical-shaped mountain. All the coast here is very rocky, but the sides of the hills, as usual, are covered with vegetation and trees.

During this day we passed a Japanese vessel, rigged up, as far as we could discern, in European fashion. Our captain gave orders to salute her, and accordingly the flag was hoisted and lowered; but they made no reply—an omission of maritime etiquette owing, most probably, to their ignorance of nautical *politesse*.

Towards evening the pilot, perceiving that it began to grow thick and foggy, ordered the helmsman to steer towards Hiogo, the seaport of the large town of Osaka, which we were told is to be opened very soon to foreigners. Our ever-watchful captain soon detected the change, and suspecting this to be a ruse for a quiet night's rest on shore, instantly gave his command to proceed straight on. The pilot, on the plea of danger, real or imaginary, refused most determinedly to guide the vessel further that night; whereupon our commander bravely, though I must confess I thought rather hazardously, took the entire charge and risk upon himself, and, thank Providence, succeeded in conducting us in perfect safety through the thick darkness.

Next day numbers of islands differing in size and form were sighted, neared, and then left in the distance again. Towards evening we saw the Daimio's palace, called "Awarie." It is situated on very flat ground, almost approaching what might be termed a plain; but a charming background of rocky mountains and verdure-clad hills gave beauty and variety to the scene. The following day we passed the dwelling of another prince, a really singular pile of buildings, surrounded by a wall, with what from a distance appeared like turrets at regular intervals. The night which succeeded this day was a dismally dark one, and we were so close to the narrower and more dangerous parts of the Suonada, that even the captain dared not venture further. We therefore anchored at an early hour in the harbour of Toorosima, where, in spite of the rain, which descended in torrents, we were soon surrounded by boats from the shore; some laden with fish, and others with fruit, which their occupants eagerly ol for sale. Empty bottles were soon, as usual, committed to the waves, which the natives dived for, substituting them for cargo, as their fish and fruit were quickly disposed of.

It was a very pretty harbour, with a fine range of hills, at the base of which was the picturesque residence of a Daimio. Had the sky been less dark and lowering, no doubt it would have appeared to still greater advantage, but as it was, I could not help thinking that, like the "monks of old," the Daimios knew well where to pitch their tents, for every residence we saw was in a most lovely situation, and in a richly fertile neighbourhood.

Soon after daylight we were ready "again to seek the watery waste." Passing first between the islands of Nipon and Sikok, about half-past ten we came in sight of a vast portion of the territories of the Daimio who supplies Yeddo and Yokohama with soldiers for their garrisons. We could distinguish, however, but little of this wealthy prince's land, through the rain, which fell like a veil between us and the shore.

That night we again anchored, for, like its predecessor, it was one of gloom and wretchedness, to be succeeded by a morning as dark and wet. Towards the afternoon the weather slightly cleared up, and about two P.M. we were passing through scenery which was enchanting beyond description. In another hour, as far as I can remember, we were entering the Straits of Simonosaki. This was indeed a day to be marked down as a memorable one in the annals of our lives. Placed in circumstances of considerable difficulty, we had experienced much doubt and uneasiness, but now rejoiced in the Providential escape with which we had been favoured.

Here the islands of Nipon and Kiusiu are in very close vicinity to each other, there being only about three hundred yards between them. Every hill, every spot, presented a most lovely verdant appearance. We had already passed one village to the right, and were approaching another on the opposite shore, when the captain, anxious to avoid a very strong current, which he knew to exist towards the middle of the passage, ordered the vessel to be steered near to the coast of Kiusiu, which commenced here to be more precipitous, the verdant tree-clad sides giving place near the water to sharp and threatening rocks.

At first all went well. The chain was arranged for the anchor to be lowered at a moment's notice, and the men, stationed at their proper places, were ready for any emergency, when, just as we arrived before a temple situated amidst luxuriant overhanging trees, the current seized the bows of the vessel (her stern being still in calm water), and in a minute swung her partially round. The large steamer, apparently powerless against the terrible force of the water, was in such close proximity to the coast, that we could clearly distinguish the marks of alarm and anxiety in the faces of the Japanese on shore, who had been for some time regarding our movements with evident interest, doubtless setting us down in their own minds as rash and heedless, for not waiting till the violent force of the stream had somewhat abated.

We must have been inevitably dashed against the rocks,* but for the astonishing coolness

---

* One of our fellow-passengers called this part Biscuit Point, because, he said, we might have thrown a biscuit far on shore.

and presence of mind our captain displayed. "Stop her!" "Let go the anchor!" "Lower the mainsail!" were the directions uttered by his clear voice, accompanied by others I now remember no longer. The only other sounds heard on board were the rattling of the cable and the furling of the sail. No commotion, no excitement, betrayed the imminent peril we all well knew we were in, but we looked at each other, and then at the vessel's bows, which swung to and fro until we had backed some distance, and were free of the current.

The forethought and precaution of the captain saved us, and the rapid noiseless way in which his orders were executed spoke volumes for the discipline of the crew. There was indeed, I remember, one exception to the general good order and regularity, which, however, we never heard of till all was over, a proof of the ease with which disobedience was checked, as, had it not been so, we must have noticed some disturbance. One sailor refused to obey an order given by the third mate, and, spite of the unfitness of the time, proving very rebellious, he was immediately carried below and put in irons, the men who had taken him returning to the deck in a few minutes again to resume their duties. After all danger was over, I believe the man was liberated, but when the crew received each an additional supply of grog for their hard labour, none was given to him—probably a more bitter punishment for his fault, the captain said, than any he could inflict.

How thankful all must have felt for this Providential escape! The depth of gratitude in each heart heaven only knew; but I think it is such moments as these that teach us, above all things, how small and insignificant we are, and how great He—Our Father—is!

After waiting some hours until the current had subsided, we steamed onward, soon cleared Biscuit Point, and, unimpeded by any further obstacle or danger, passed the town of Simonosaki, which lay to our right. It is a very large straggling place, situated at the base of a long range of low hills, on the island of Nipon, and is said to extend three miles along the coast. Were it open to foreigners, it would doubtless prove a most advantageous port for European merchants.

The harbour, in which we saw a number of junks lying at anchor, is large, well sheltered, and very attractive, from the mountains and hills by which it is encompassed. It is considered a very wealthy place, and being on the high road to Yeddo, every Japanese or Korean from Kiusiu or the Korea, generally stops there for rest before he commences his journey to the capital. It contains a great many godowns and commercial houses, one Prince's residence, and an endless number of temples.

The native trade with the neighbouring coasts and Korea is very extensive. All travellers from the opposite or Kiusiu side are ferried across to Simonosaki from the little village of Kokura. One of the Daimios has a very beautiful house here. A fine long avenue of straight trees, which can be seen bordering the river's edge for a long distance westward, denotes the highway from Nagasaki. This road, as far as has been seen by Europeans, is always most carefully kept in order, the large trees with which it is regularly planted forming a delightful shelter from sun or rain.

When we were fairly out of the straits, which is from four to five miles in length, I should think, we took a northerly direction, and dropped anchor in a quiet little bay for the night. It was a pretty spot, like a lake enclosed by a few small islands closely grouped together. The night, which was finer than we had enjoyed of late, admitted of our spending a few agreeable hours on deck before retiring. Unfortunately the fair weather was of very short duration, for the next morning we again opened our eyes to a watery sky. It was with regret we left our snug retreat, for the atmosphere grew thicker and heavier, and the drenching rain and violent winds which succeeded obliged us to tack about and alter our course so frequently that at last our captain, after a day of great anxiety, determined to seek some place of refuge.

Accordingly we made for the harbour of Toorumchibukoo, where although we could plainly see from the distance what a fearful tempest raged outside, we passed a moderately calm night.

Two officials came on board from the village or town, put the usual questions, and appeared satisfied with the replies they elicited. We were informed by them that, owing to the stormy state of the weather, no fishing junk had put to sea for three days—a fact which accounted for the absence of fish for sale. The captain invited them into the saloon, and offered each a glass of curaçoa, with which they were so delighted that they begged for the gift of the whole bottle. This request was immediately granted, and they both emptied the contents of their inexhausted glasses into the bottle, and corked it up, afraid, I suppose, of taking too much at one time of such a delicate luxury. When they left the ship they expressed the utmost satisfaction at the reception they had received. This harbour is excessively pretty, the hills around very woody, and the country bright and green.

The following morning, soon after day-break, we were off again, passing islands with low hills and undulating plains, and very soon entering the beautiful straits of Herado or Spexis. The land to the right, with the line of distant hills, is part of the Island of Kiusiu, whilst those cliffs to the left, and the hill on which, embedded in luxuriant foliage, a Daimio's house is situated, is that of Hirado. The weather still continued very bad, and there was a frequent cry of "breakers ahead!" "rocks!" &c., until we reached Nagasaki next morning, to the delight of every one on board, and to the inexpressible relief of the captain, with whom the principal care and anxiety had rested.

We now stayed in another part of the European quarter of Nagasaki, with friends whose hospitality equalled any we had yet received. Though we had no letter of introduction to them, and were perfect strangers to each other, they treated us as if we had been old and valued friends. Their house was beautifully situated on a hill, commanding a fine view of the entrance as well as of the interior of the harbour.

During our stay this time, we went, by express invitation, to the house of a wealthy Japanese merchant. We found him surrounded by friends and relatives, ready to receive us. He was a burly-looking individual, with a pleasant, good-humoured expression of countenance, and a very affable manner. His wife was, apparently, some years younger, an active body, and very solicitous that we should partake amply of the repast prepared for us. This consisted of a very good kind of sponge-cake, together with other confectionary, and the usual beverage of tea, without milk or sugar, milk being a liquid not used as an article for human consumption in Japan. These were placed on a box, which was covered by a red cloth, and arranged for us as a substitute for a table. They had likewise been at the trouble of obtaining chairs from some European house, as they themselves eat, drink, sit, and sleep on the floor.

We were much amused by our visit, and, on taking our departure, agreed to accompany the good people to the theatre next day. The wife, with some of her friends, accompanied us back, as she was most anxious to see our little girl, with whom she was so enraptured that she actually begged me as a favour to allow her to keep the child for a few days, an invitation which, I need hardly say, we politely declined.

As our friends had a piano, I played and sung for them several airs, with which they seemed quite astonished, probably never having heard the instrument before. I observed a young Yacoonin particularly attentive, who regarded my fingers with the deepest interest. On my rising up, he immediately took possession of the chair I had just vacated, exclaiming, in a confident tone, "Have got! have got!" and commencing to hammer on the keys without mercy, he produced, as may be well imagined, more discord than melody. This he continued for some seconds, when, finding the sounds created by himself not so harmonious as mine, he gave up further trial, fully convinced the art required a little more study than he at first thought.

I often longed very much to be able to speak the Japanese language, which I thought rather a pretty one. The natives, too, whom I met, who were always very affable, seemed particularly pleased when I endeavoured to put a few of their words together. They welcomed us wherever we went with smiling countenances, and not unfrequently gave us tea, the women at the same time offering me their own pipes and tobacco pouches, judging by themselves that I should like " a puff," and expressing the utmost astonishment at my refusal to

> " Enjoy the weed
> Through a bamboo reed."

Their salutation on meeting each other is very peculiar. They bow nearly to the ground, and on parting, place a hand on each of their own thighs, and as they bow slide it along until it reaches the knee, drawing a long deep inhalation all the time, and concluding by the familiar word "sionara."

The day of our departure we went to the Japanese theatre, a temporary shed, the part where the audience sat being supported by stout poles, and the roof covered with matting. The boxes were on each side, in two tiers, one immediately above the other. Into the highest we mounted by means of a ladder, and joined the merchant's wife and family, who had engaged it for the day. The performance had long commenced, as the doors open early in the morning, and close at six P.M. When we arrived the drop scene was down, from which we concluded that one act was finished, and therefore the interval allowed us ample time to take a look round the house. The drop scene was a very gay one, representing an enormous tiger, gaudily painted, in a jungle of very bluish-coloured bamboo. The pit is divided into squares, each capable of holding from nine to ten persons. These are generally occupied by a whole family, who pay four itziboos and a half (about nine shillings) for the compartment, in which they spend the entire day, making it a regular holiday, a servant bringing their food at appointed hours in chow-chow, or food boxes.

On one side of the pit a walk is formed by planks joined together, on which the actors and actresses come in and go out, when they do not wish to do so by the sides of the stage. At the back of the pit was a kind of raised platform for labourers and their families.

Our "box" was on the left side, and opposite to us, partially concealed by a curtain, were seated those who constituted the orchestra, namely, two banjo players and one drummer. Before them sat a fat, flabby-looking individual, whose air of importance and subsequent manœuvres bespoke him at once to be a prompter, fully aware of the responsibility resting on his shoulders. Immediately in front of him was a long board, on which he hammered with a deafening noise, to announce the entrance or exit of any performer, or on which he made the colophon, or conclusion, to any extra-pathetic or energetic passage of the drama.

Now the klack-ka-ta-klack sounds are heard, and the curtain is drawn aside, disclosing a woman seated, or rather kneeling, with the curious kind of stool I have before described, for her to rest her back upon. She is very gaily attired, in the usual loose dress, to which, however, she has added a very long train, worn by all ladies of rank in Japan. Her hair is ornamented with an endless amount of pins and beads, and the powder on her face looks more like a thin covering of white muslin than any powdering I ever saw before. There is no deceit here, no attempt at *slight* improvement to the complexion, but the white looks as thick as paint, and the effect produced is very ghastly. The dress of the man, too, in the play, with the exception of a small cape, and a greater variety of colours, is similar to that generally worn.

From what I could gather of the plot, it seemed to be a serio-comic drama, the tale evidently being one of desperate jealousy.

The lady whom we first see is an unfortunately jealous wife, who fancies her husband has fallen in love with another woman. She does not openly upbraid him for his unfaithfulness, but seeks redress from high quarters, and as she is evidently related to influential people, her appeal is not made in vain. The unlucky offender is apprehended, and condemned to be decapitated, unless he saves himself the ignominy of a public execution by committing the hara-kari. Unwilling to be thus disgraced, he consents to this self-immolation. All is prepared, friends, relatives, and spectators assemble to witness the melancholy sight. They only await the arrival of the doomed man, who is carried on to the stage in a Norimon. Some time is supposed to have elapsed since the audience last saw him, and in the interval, according to the custom on such mournful occasions, his hair has been suffered to grow, so that, on leaving the Norimon, he stands quite conspicuous amidst his shaven brethren.

Every one appears absorbed in watching this scene, perfect silence reigns around, broken only by the voices from the stage, which seem to come slowly and half-whispered. At this moment a commotion is heard outside, a heart-rending cry disturbs the general tranquillity, the wife rushes into the place, and, uttering some words, totters forward in a manner which proves her intention of falling, when, fortunately, the extended arms of her lord and master save her, and she triumphantly exhibits to the husband whom her jealousy had wrongfully accused, the order for his freedom, which she had herself sought for, and with difficulty obtained in time.

CHAPTER XII.

RETURN TO SHANGHAE—VOYAGE TO HONG KONG—TYPHOON—WE PUT IN AT AMOY—GO ASHORE THERE—TAME CHINESE TIGER—DISMASTED SHIPS ENTERING THE PORT—DEATH OF A CHINAMAN ON BOARD—SINGULAR REQUEST OF HIS FRIENDS—SAFE ARRIVAL AT VICTORIA—TYPHOON THERE—ANOTHER PEEP AT MACAO—WE GO TO CANTON—PAGODAS—BODIES FLOATING DOWN THE STREAM—INTENSE HEAT—JOSS HOUSE—SINGULAR MONUMENT FOR AN ENGLISH SAILOR—ILLUMINATED BOATS ON THE RIVER—RETURN TO VICTORIA—FEAST OF LANTERNS—CURIOUS SUBSTITUTE FOR MACHINERY.

CHAPTER XII.

It was not without regret that we bade adieu to Nagasaki, where we had spent so many pleasant hours, and the beauty of which so much delighted our eye; but "time is ever on the wing," and if we did not avail ourselves of the opportunity now offered by the departure of the steamer, we might have very long to wait for another.

We did not stay many days at Shanghae on this our second and last visit, but took our passage on the 18th of July, in the steamer *Lyeemoon*. We proceeded on our voyage at a capital rate until the third day, when, about eleven o'clock, a violent storm commenced. To us it appeared to come on quite suddenly, but the captain fully expected it, as the glass had been falling rapidly since very early in the morning, and the sky had presented all the usual presages of a storm "brewing aloft."

As we were not far from Amoy, we put back and entered the harbour, only just in time to escape the greatest violence of the typhoon, which had now set in with all its terrible fury, and continued unabated till next morning. Our mainmast was lowered, and the awning taken down, to steady our vessel during the force of the tempest. Thus, whilst the winds blew from all quarters, and the sky, dark and lowering, poured down torrents of rain, we lay perfectly snug and comfortable at anchor, our only danger being the possibility that some other vessel might be driven from her moorings and come in violent contact with us *en passant*. This, however, I am thankful to say, we escaped.

We were by no means sorry at the chance of thus seeing another port, and one which, though insignificant by comparison, was still very interesting; but the captain regretted the necessary delay, and often said that this was the first time his vessel had been compelled to take shelter from stress of weather. We did not leave next day, though it was calm, as the captain thought it more advisable to wait. It was too wet, however, for us to dream of going on shore, much as we wished to do so. We had, therefore, only to hope for fairer weather before we started, to enable us to take a peep at Amoy.

That night a Chinese second-class passenger died, and his friends or relatives, I know not which, came requesting the captain to give them some brandy for the dead man. Though he could scarcely suppress a smile at the singularity of the demand, he kindly complied with their request. This is only in accordance with what I have before heard, that they try all kinds of plans to revive the dead man, frequently placing even money in his mouth. The sailors intended to throw the body into the sea, but to this his friends objected, as we were so near shore, and begged the captain's permission to carry it with them in a boat, and bury it in their cemetery near Amoy.

Early the following morning we left the vessel on an exploring expedition, in a little boat rowed by an old Chinaman, and glad was I to see oars in use once more, instead of the jogging process of sculling.

The Chinese town is situated on the island of Amoy, at the foot of a bare-looking ridge of hills. This island is very picturesque, and close to the main land. The European officers and godowns are here, but for the most part they fix their residences in the opposite island, a narrow strip of land, with rugged rocks peeping out here and there amid the green turf. The houses are mostly constructed in a pretty light style, which accords well with the general character of the scene. A little to the right is a small island, with a tower-like building on it, which was formerly a signal place for pirates.

In the town we first visited the dock, which is about a hundred and forty-five yards long by twenty-five broad. There was only one old vessel in it, and there seemed room for another. The next place we went to see was the Roman Catholic Church, the interior of which was a slight degree more simple than these churches generally are. We observed, however, three very gaudy-looking images, before which some devotees were praying.

We found the town very dirty—a perfect swamp—from the recent storm. The streets, as usual, were so narrow that one could jump with ease from the roof of one house to that opposite.

A gentleman took us to see a young tiger, between six and seven months old, which was so tame that it followed him about like a dog, and seemed quite pleased when we patted his head. The gentleman told us he paid ten dollars for him when he was first caught, a few months prior to the time we saw him, and that he had now sold him to the English Consul for a hundred pounds. I believe it is intended for the Zoological Gardens in London, where it will figure as the first from China ever seen there, and where we may some day renew our acquaintance with the tiger of Amoy.

We returned to the *Lyeemoon* well pleased with our little excursion, and as we glanced around at the numerous vessels now in the harbour for shelter, and others coming in, we could not but feel deep thankfulness in contrasting our state with theirs. Some were almost mastless, others with rudder broken and bulwarks entirely gone. One arrived just before our departure in almost a complete state of wreck. It was towed into harbour by an English gun-boat, and the faces of the poor crew were really pitiable to behold—they presented such a pale, careworn look.

Soon after mid-day we left our moorings, and were quickly steaming far from Amoy. Numbers of small rocks are scattered all about the mouth of this harbour, the source of imminent danger to inexperienced seamen. It would have been utterly impossible for us to secure this safe retreat had we not most fortunately been so near when the storm began, and thus able to enter before the "stiff and chopping winds" commenced to blow.

Soon after our arrival in Victoria we were again honoured with a typhoon. This time, however, we were on land, and felt more secure, though it happened at night, precluding all possibility of sleeping, by the terrific noise it made. The wind appeared to blow all round the house, and at times it really seemed as if one was not safe in bed. Some accidents occurred, but few in comparison to the fearful loss of life that happened almost simultaneously at Canton and Macao. The mortality in the former place was estimated at about eight or ten thousand, and in the latter seven hundred souls. Thirty cargo boats were thrown high and dry, some on the Isla Verde, others near the harbour, some on the isthmus, and others, again, on the beach of the main land.

We revisited Macao two days after this disastrous storm, and could not suppress a smile when we saw the boat people living in their boats on the Praya Grande. The whole of the old harbour presented a picture of ruin and disorder. Here we saw a boat sunk and unclaimed, the poor owners having probably drifted into eternity; there a large junk upside down, the mast thrust through its side, and numbers of planks, boxes, and bodies floating about.

The Praya Grande was two or three feet thick with an accumulation of bricks, stones, clay, and mud. The chopping winds of the typhoon, so termed from veering from one quarter of the compass to another, had not been idle. Tiles were swept down from the housetops, thick as hail-stones, and rickety venetians and flowerpots were dashed to atoms. The scene, as presented to our eyes, seemed a dismal sequel to a terrible earthquake, or, in the words of a Portuguese poet,

"Um resto infeliz de terremoto."

After a few days pleasantly spent at Macao, we left for Canton, in one of the steamers plying twice a week between these two places. The voyage took us between eight and nine hours, and would have been very agreeable but for the oppressive heat of the weather. We passed the Bocca Tigris at the entrance to the Canton river. This famous fort, or rather, I should say, high battery, is situated at the foot of a very high, precipitous hill. It is semicircular in form, and has embrasures for guns facing the water, while its two side walls, almost uniting in a point behind, afford an excellent protection for the occupants in case of siege. They tried hard, during the first and second Chinese wars, to oppose our entrance by this fort, which, with a European garrison, might be made almost impregnable, owing to its favourable position. During the last war our Sikhs took it by storm, and slaughtered, without mercy, all found within the walls.

All this part bears marks of having been

strongly fortified, but all alike shew how ineffectual were the powers of resistance used. In the first war the Chinese fixed a chain of about two miles in length from the fort to a small rock opposite, thinking thus most effectually to debar the entrance of any man-of-war; but, to their no small consternation, this barrier was speedily removed by the gun-boats sent ahead for that purpose.

Beyond this the scenery began to grow very pretty. The paddy fields were green, and continued, with but little interruption, all the way up to Whampoa, beyond which there were hills with little villages here and there, and very frequently a Pagoda, with its many stories, presenting not an unpleasing appearance as it rose high above hillocks and mounds. Some assert that they were erected to serve as landmarks, while others maintain that they were "sign posts," denoting the division of one Prince's territory from that of his neighbour. Many of them appear to be very ancient, and are partially covered with creepers.

At Whampoa there are a great number of docks, but owing to the late typhoon the ravages in every direction were fearful to look upon.

The bodies of several of the unfortunate sufferers were still to be seen floating about, though some had been collected and buried. Many, probably the greater number, had been borne out by the tide to the great deep.

Whampoa is considered a rising place. It is incredible how many have made a large and speedy fortune here in the building and repairing of ships. It is to Whampoa that every Spanish vessel is sent from Manilla to be altered or refitted, as the short-sightedness of the citizens of the latter place has led them to put off the construction of a dock to this day.

The next object of interest we passed was the Dutch Folly, not far from Canton. This was a fort, situated on an island in the middle of the river. Why it received this name I cannot say, unless it was from having been built by the Dutch in such an exposed situation. Only a few stones now remain to mark the spot, or to show that a wall was once built all round.

The unartistic appearance of this large flat town now at once strikes the visitor. Clusters of houses are seen in all directions, crowded close upon each another, without any regard to regularity or beauty of architecture; and the eye seeks in vain, amidst this forest of roofs, "for some green leaf to rest upon."

We anchored about a mile beyond the Dutch Folly, and landed "streaming with perspiration," and sick with the fearful heat and close odours exhaling both from the dense masses of houses on land and from those built on flat boats on the water.

I do not remember, during our stay in Canton, to have seen a single carriage either there or in Honam—one of the suburbs of the town. As chairs and boats are the usual, in fact, the sole means of conveyance, we made use of the former by day to see the sights and make purchases, and the latter by night, when we wished to enjoy a slightly cooler temperature, for it was impossible to walk, the heat in the house never being less than 98° Fahrenheit night or day.

Here, too, the typhoon had caused terrible ruin and destruction, though much had been done already to remedy the disaster, and to restore things to the condition in which they were previous to this fatal visitation.

The streets of Canton are, as usual in

Chinese towns, "long and unlovely," and the shops abound in the ordinary run of goods, fancy and useful. Canton, I believe, is not the proper name of the town, for that given to it by the Chinese sounds something like Kaan-choo-fow. The division of the country of which it is the capital is called Kaan-long. Whether the Europeans have formed the name Canton from that of the provinces is a point in dispute, but seems to me not unlikely. The town is situated on two rivers, the Chow-Kaun and the Pi-Kaun, and is computed to lie between thirty-two and thirty-three miles inland.

We visited some of the joss-houses, one of which is said to contain five hundred images. It is a curious place, for you have to thread your way through corridors lined with figures in various forms, costumes, and attitudes. Our guide pointed to one which he called the Ying-ki-li-god. Most singular to say, it was the figure of a European, conspicuous amidst the crowd of others by the sailor's hat which is on his head, the ruff round his neck, the cloak on the shoulders, and still further by a thick beard, an appendage which no Chinese seems to appreciate. I learnt subsequently that this gilt image had been placed there in memory of an English sailor who was shipwrecked on the Chinese coast, picked up by the natives, and cruelly imprisoned. During this unkind treatment he displayed much patient endurance, and being a clever mechanic and an ingenious man, he bethought himself of a means by which he might win the favour of his keepers, by presenting them with some article he contrived to make, which proving quite a novelty to the celestials, they crowded to the prison to see a man of such wonderful genius. His fame spread so far that it even reached the Governor of that part of the country, who, appreciating the talent of the poor captive, ordered his release. He even came in person to satisfy his curiosity, and was so prepossessed by the appearance of our countryman, that he at once made him a mandarin, and loaded him with honours. These favours continued until his death, when, to testify their respect for his memory, the image I have before alluded to was placed in the temple.

Our visit being during the month of August, we saw numbers of boats nightly on the river covered with lanterns hung from the sides and rigging, which, with their reflections, had a very pretty effect. We also saw them frequently throw lighted papers into the water. These they watch with great anxiety, until they are extinguished, believing that the longer the paper continues lighted, the more lucky they will be. This, we were told, was their " feast of lanterns."

The origin of this annual feast it is difficult to arrive at, but one legend in connection with it I have seen quoted by Moore, in a note of his "Lalla Rooke," which, for the benefit of those who have not read that poem, I may insert here: "The vulgar ascribe it to an accident that happened in the family of a famous mandarin, whose daughter, walking one evening upon the shore of a lake, fell in and was drowned. The afflicted father, with his family, ran thither, and the better to find her, he caused a great company of lanterns to be lighted. All the inhabitants of the place thronged after him with torches. The year ensuing they made fires upon the shore the same day. They continued the ceremony every year—every one lighted his lantern, and by degrees it commenced into a custom."

EXHIBITION OF CLAY FIGURES. 295

We were glad when all the sights were exhausted, and our time to leave approached, for the heat was intolerable, and our rest at night was broken and disturbed, in consequence of the fearful closeness of the atmosphere.

At Hong Kong, previous to leaving, we went to see a Chinese exhibition of clay figures, in celebration of the feast of lanterns. We had already seen a similar one at Macao, but this was on a much grander scale. It was held in a large temporary shed, erected on the side of the mountain, to which we ascended by means of steps made of planks, a distance of about sixty or seventy feet from the road. The whole affair was very ingenious and magnificent, and must have cost an enormous sum—some said, indeed, fully twenty thousand dollars, which were raised by subscription.

The interior was brilliantly illuminated with lamps in every imaginable form, colour, and device. Flowers hung in festoons from the roof, and formed fantastic groups in various directions, whilst orange trees, the camelia, and other floral ornaments, were arranged with so much taste that the place presented quite an attractive appearance. The aroma from some of them however, proved a little too powerful for the densely crowded place.

The principal attraction consisted of figures made of clay, mostly in large cases, arranged in groups or tableaux to represent various interesting scenes, warlike as well as domestic. These, by a very simple contrivance, were made to roll their eyes, and to raise the head, hand, leg, or body, in accordance with the action they were meant to illustrate.

The portions of each figure intended to move were attached behind to thin wires, the ends of which were fixed to a kind of wheel, and the whole being enclosed within boards forming a sort of box, one or more white mice were introduced into it, who, whenever they touched the wheel, or traversed it, caused the action desired in the figures forming the tableaux. We all thought this an excellent plan, for the effect produced was occasional, not continuous, and looked far more natural than the precise regularity of machinery otherwise worked. Sometimes these little prisoners would escape from their confinement, and run about amidst the group of figures in a bewildered manner, forming a lively addition to the scene.

And now, gentle readers, "my work is done." Trusting that it has at least succeeded in whiling away a portion of your time, if it has proved a means neither of instruction nor of information, I will lay my pen aside, and, making my exit from your mind, say Adieu!

THE END.

LONDON: PRINTED BY MACDONALD AND TUGWELL, BLENHEIM HOUSE.

www.ingramcontent.com/pod-product-compliance
Lightning Source LLC
Chambersburg PA
CBHW022050230426
43672CB00008B/1132